'IF I REMEMB

'IF I REMEMBER RIGHTLY...'

Roger Ordish

see next page →

YouCaxton Publications
Oxford & Shrewsbury

Copyright © Roger Ordish 2019
The Author asserts the moral right to
be identified as the author of this work.
ISBN 978-1-913425-11-1

Published by YouCaxton Publications 2020
YCBN: 01

All rights reserved. No part of this publication may be reproduced, stored in a retrieval system, or transmitted in any form or by any means, electronic, mechanical, photocopying, recording or otherwise, without the prior permission of the author.
This book is sold subject to the condition that it shall not, by way of trade or otherwise, be lent, resold, hired out or otherwise circulated without the author's prior consent in any form of binding or cover other than that in which it is published and without a similar condition including this condition being imposed on the subsequent purchaser.

YouCaxton Publications

enquiries@youcaxton.co.uk

For Lulu

With love from
the author,
also known as Daddy

xx

CONTENTS

Foreword ix
1. BE BRAVE 1
2. THE 1940s 7
3. FAMILY 11
4. I.Q. 14
5. TONBRIDGE 19
6. SCHOOL 22
7. SPORT AT SCHOOL 26
8. SCHOOL CORPS 29
9. ACTING 33
10. GAP YEARS 36
11. DUBLIN 40
12. VIRGIN TRANSATLANTIC 48
13. ORTHOMORPHIC MYCORRHIZA 55
14. BBC RADIO 57
15. RICHMOND, SURREY 62
16. BBC TELEVISION 64
17. CHELSEA 70
18. SONG CONTEST 73
19. PUBS ETC. 76
20. BACKWARDS 78
21. PROGRAMMES 84
22. MORE CHAT 88

23. SAVILE	92
24. BEGINNING OF THE END	94
25. FIXTURES AND FITTINGS	102
26. MRS THATCHER	113
27. SPECTRA	119
28. DE LUXE	122
29. ENTERTAINMENT	127
30. POLITICS	134
31. PERNICKETY	140
32. ODD ONE OUT	144
33. SECRETS	148
34. WORDS, WORDS. WORDS	150
35. LEWES	153
36. OPERATICS	159
37. FRANCE	161
38. MEDICINE	163
39. BREXIT LEFT	165
40. RICHMOND, YORKSHIRE	167
41. AND FINALLY	168
List of Illustrations	170
Acknowledgements	174

FOREWORD

I have just turned eighty. Is it too late to get some memories down on paper or into some kind of e-book? I hope not. My father had at least one book published, when he was in his eighties and was in the middle of writing another, when he died aged eighty-seven in 1991. I do not imagine that these ramblings will be seized upon by a publisher but, ignoring the insult implied, I shall settle for 'vanity publishing'. I hope that family, friends and former colleagues might like to read these words in one form or another.

With regard to source material, I did occasionally make diary entries over the years. Generally my good intentions lasted only a few days. The earliest diary entry I can find was when I was seven and we children were all keen on our scooters. In proper diarist style, omitting the first person singular, I wrote:

'Scooted in morning, mucked about in afternoon'.

I no longer scoot but I do still muck about.

1.

BE BRAVE

One of my earliest memories is having my hair washed by my mother and making a fuss about it. She told me to stop fussing and to be brave. I hope I was. Earlier than that, I am told that I was crying in my pram as the result of distant explosions. My elder sister comforted me, saying, "Don't cry, baby. It's only bombs." I know that my first words were 'all clear', the name of the siren sounded at the end of an air raid alert. We lived in a village called Yalding in Kent. My parents must have worried continuously about the state of the war. A German invasion would almost certainly have arrived in Kent and we were underneath the flight path for German bombers on their way to London. I remember my mother telling me later that she had an emergency evacuation plan, which would have involved bundling her two babies, my elder sister and me, into a pram. Quite where she would have taken the pram, I cannot imagine. Not that I remember the event, of course, being not yet one year old, but we were right underneath the Battle of Britain in 1940. The village doctor's son was a pilot in that conflict and survived it. On his way home from a sortie, Flight Lieutenant Toddy Hallam D.F.C. would 'buzz' his mother's house, diving to a few feet above her with tremendous din, to let her know he was on his way back safely to nearby West Malling airfield. Later he was taken prisoner after crashing in France and spent the rest of the war in a 'Stalag' somewhere. His capture was probably the reason that he survived the war and it seemed so very unfair that he was killed in 1952 on a training flight, in which his pupil is believed to have panicked, bringing them both to their untimely deaths. His widow and two young sons, Martin and Ian, lived opposite our house. Ian was about four and confused my name with that of another local boy, who was called Robert. Ian Hallam referred to me as Rogert. His elder brother, Martin, was very proud of his first ever necktie. Arriving in our house wearing it one day, he asked my mother, "Would you like to know how long my tie is?". "Yes," she replied, "How long is your tie, Martin?" He paused for a moment and then said, "Very".

One day, when I was four years old. My two sisters and I were playing with plasticine in the nursery, when there was a deafening bang and some of the ceiling fell down. It turned out that one of the first of the Nazis' new secret weapon, the V2 flying bomb, had exploded in marshy ground the other side of an orchard opposite our house.

The V2, successor to the 'Doodlebugs', travelled too fast to be intercepted by the R.A.F. Even the V.1 Doodlebugs with their pulse jet engines travelled faster than the Royal Air Force's Spitfires and Hurricanes, but the brave pilots used to line themselves up ahead of the advancing, pilotless aircraft and try to upset the bomb by disturbing the airflow over its wings as it overtook them. If they were successful, the flying bombs - instead of going on to highly-populated London - would land to the east of the town - for example in the countryside, where we lived. You can't have everything.

We were none of us seriously hurt and I can remember visiting the site of the crater left by the V2. I picked up a bit of bluish metal, part of the bomb, as a souvenir, but to my great disappointment had to hand it over at the orchard gate to a policeman, who must have been under instructions to collect any evidence he could about this unknown new weapon.

Going back to Doodlebugs, the name was to some extent onomatopoeic, the 'doodle' represented the rat-a-tat tat of their pulse jet engines. It was known that, when this noise stopped, the craft was out of fuel and would immediately dive almost vertically downwards and detonate its explosive on hitting the ground. People waiting nervously in their air-raid shelters knew that, when a Doodlebug engine cut out, a huge explosion would shortly follow. My godfather, Sir Edward Hardy, was chairman of the Kent County Council and was delighted to learn after the war that he had been named personally on the Nazis' hit list for extermination following a successful German invasion. One afternoon, he was sitting at his desk at home in Chilham, Kent, when there was a knock at his study door. His maid, Alice, entered the room and said, "Excuse me, Sir Edward, but the engine has stopped." As she said the word 'stopped', there was a massive explosion and some of the windows were blown in. Neither person was injured and I have a wonderful picture in my mind of bits of plaster and papers from my godfather's desk fluttering to the floor in the ensuing chaos and my godfather peering through a cloud of settling dust, his collar askew and saying calmly, "Thank you, Alice. That will be all."

Some sixty years later I made a short film for an organisation called 'Heroes' Return', who arranged trips for ex-servicemen to visit the scenes of their wartime experiences. I filmed a party of ex-RAF aircrew, who visited a V-2 factory and launch-pad, known as 'La Coupole' near Saint Omer in northern France. Many years earlier these brave men had flown through heavy flak in their efforts to destroy this almost bomb-proof bunker.

I also remember an amoured troop carrier full of soldiers stopping outside our front gate one day. I was watching them and suddenly decided they must be Germans. I was terrified. Then one of the soldiers came over to me and said 'hello' in what was clearly English. I noticed that he had cut his hand, which was bleeding. I remember thinking he must be brave, because he wasn't making a fuss.

Although paying school fees out of income put quite a strain on my parents' budget, some of the aspects of our life then seem to belong to a different age. We had a maid, who wore a uniform and addressed my mother as 'Madam'. My father, who had suffered from tuberculosis as a child, was not accepted for military service, although I can remember his black tin helmet inscribed 'W' for 'warden', showing that he served on a volunteer air raid patrol. He was also in what was called a 'reserved occupation', employed by I.C.I. in their agricultural division. Before the war he had worked in France, on occasions advising wine growers on pest control. That gave him a lifelong interest in grape growing and he was determined to prove that good wine could be made from grapes grown in the open air in England. My mother was not always sure about the 'good' aspect of the wine he produced. However, the Romans had done it; why should not we? Eventually all but the north side of the house was covered in grape vines and more grew on trellises in the garden. At his most ambitious my father, in addition to the sixty gallons of red and white wine he produced, made some bottles of sparkling wine produced by the champagne method. This is a highly skilled process. Fermented wine has to undergo a sugar-induced secondary fermentation in its bottles. During this process my father would store the bottles upside down, so that any sediment would drift downwards on to the cork. Before the fermentation is complete, the bottles have to be briefly uncorked to remove the sediment and re-corked allowing fermentation to continue in the clear wine. If there was too much sugar, or if the fermentation was too powerful, the bottles would explode and I can remember hearing from time to time explosions from one of the outhouses where the sparkling wine was developing. One of the many books my father wrote was, 'Wine Growing in England', whose front cover showed an eight-year-old me operating the wine press. (*illustration*).

His interest in alcohol did not stop at wine. As children we were sometimes sent out to pick sloes. I don't think I ever asked what the sloes were for. We never seemed to eat them. Much later I was to learn that they were used to take away the filthy taste of the bathtub gin that he and a work colleague would distil clandestinely in the local I.C.I. laboratory.

My father was a kind and gentle man, generous and hardworking. I do not think I realised how much I loved him until his death in 1991. A slight compensation was to see his obituary in 'the Times'. It was good to know that his talents, which he tended to hide under a bushel, had been recognised.

My first school was St Christopher's 'pre-prep' in Maidstone. It was originally for boys and girls, but, as the years progressed, the preponderance was for girls. That meant that parents started taking their boys away from the school, preferring somewhere with a balance of genders. But, since my elder sister was already there and my younger sister was to follow, it did not make sense to send us to different schools. I ended with a year as the only boy in the school. That did not make much difference to me, since I had two sisters and was used to the monstrous regiment of women. The only distinction was that I had exclusive use of the boys' lavatory.

Most memorable at St. Christopher's were the rudimentary French lessons, which started when the pupils were only five years old. The girls and I sat round a table, on which were several pictorial cards. In turn we had to ask Miss Paffard, the headmistress, in French, which card we wanted. There were no genders; everything, like my fellow pupils, was feminine. Neither was there any attempt at a French accent. This is how I remember the routine: "Donny wah, sill voo play lah table" or "Donny wah, sill voo play lah veston." Even the man was feminine. If you requested his card, you would say, "Donny wah sill voo play lah l'homme."

We went regularly to Sunday School, where we sang "Hear the Pennies Drop in. Listen while they fall, Every one for Jesus, He shall have them all", while the vicar, Mr Howlden, bumped his hymn book gently in time with the music on the heads of those in the first pew. The wise thing to do was avoid the front row.

I felt honoured, when, aged five or six I was chosen to hold up the big brass plate at the altar during the collection of the said pennies. Unfortunately I held up the plate at the wrong time, when it was still empty, before the pennies had dropped in. I don't know what Jesus would have thought of an empty offertory plate. I was mocked by classmates for my mistiming. Shame is an emotion that stays in the memory for ever.

Later, when I was a sophisticated eleven year old, we would secretly sing, "Hear the pennies drop in, listen while they fall. Every one for Howlden (the vicar), he shall have them all"

When I was about seven, I went with my parents to Paris, where my father was on a business trip. The austerity then in Britain was for more stringent than it was in France. I had never seen real cream cakes, which abounded in Paris. Apart from the cream cakes, the only thing my diary recalls was the spectacular American cars to be seen in the Paris streets. While my parents were showing me the Louvre and les Tuileries, I was noting 'Packard V-8' or 'Buick Roadmaster' in my diary.

I like to think that it was relevant to my later career, that I was always interested in creating entertainment in one form or another for my long-suffering parents. With cardboard cut-outs or actual toy soldiers as the cast, I used to stage 'shadow shows', in which I would be the voices of various characters, whose shadows would appear on a stretched sheet, lit by a torch or candle. The dramas, as far as I can remember, were a sort of 'Dick Barton' variant. My father had a cine camera and projector, using the brilliant French Pathé 9.5 millimetre system, in which practically the whole width of the film was used as picture rather than using side sprocket holes, which is the case with 8 millimetre film. For one reason or another the Kodak eight millimetre system won, although the size of image on the newcomer was smaller than the old French system. I do not think we made movies on this equipment – too expensive, perhaps, but on odd bits of black film I would etch with a sharp point very primitive attempts at animation. A few paperbacks from my teen years still have pencil-drawn images in the bottom right hand corner of each page, which give the illusion of movement as you flick through the pages with your thumb. It probably took longer to do that than it did to read the book. The whole business reads well as 'television producer's early years'.

2.

THE 1940s

My mother's favourite cousin was Tim Denison-Smith. He had turned down the chance of a place at Brasenose College, Oxford, to join the police force in Burma. What a strange choice. When the war came, he was captured by the Japanese and incarcerated in the horrific Changi concentration camp. Somehow he survived the war, came back to England, took up his place at Oxford and became a master at the Dragon School there. I can remember his son, Anthony, visiting us in Yalding and showing great prowess at sliding down our banisters. I do not know if it is a skill that is useful in a military career, but Anthony certainly did very well in the army. After Harrow and Sandhurst he was commissioned into the Grenadier Guards, eventually becoming their colonel and on one occasion leading the ceremony of Trooping the Colour. He went on to become a general and a Knight of the Bath. On retirement from the army he was appointed Governor of the Tower of London. I wonder if he used to slide down the banisters there?

My mother was a good artist and had worked as a theatrical designer with Oliver Messel, who was then probably the top name in that business, creating costume and set design for prima ballerina (later Dame) Alicia Markova and others. In the more down-to-earth world of looking after three children she would design inn signs for Whitbread's Brewery, who preferred more obscure pub names to run-of- the mill Kings' and Queens' heads. One design I can still picture was for a pub in Tonbridge called 'the Cardinal's Error', being both a pun and a reference to the downfall of Cardinal Wolsey, whose head was the inn's sign. Whitbread issued a series of small metal cards, illustrated with their pubs' inn-signs. The idea must have been to encourage people to visit as many Whitbread pubs as possible, collecting these cards as they went. I do not know if it was a successful campaign, but I know that we children would take bike rides to various local Whitbread pubs, who would give us these cards without so much as a lemonade passing our lips.

Shortly before my eighth birthday I moved on as a dayboy to a prep school in Tonbridge. The school was run by the Bickmore brothers and was known affectionately (or unaffectionately) as 'Bickey's'. Mr. Maurice, the senior brother, was pedantic and probably sadistic, although I managed to escape his cane throughout my stay at Yardley Court. He had a habit of clearing his throat unnecessarily and the sound of his "err hem", as he approached, would fill my heart with terror. I went to a Tonbridge School reunion recently and a contemporary, Paul Thompson, who had also been at Yardley Court, stood behind me and did a perfect imitation of Mr Maurice's 'Er Hem'. Temporarily I froze.

Mr. Eric, Maurice's younger brother, was dashing and athletic. He had played cricket for Kent and usually wore his Cambridge 'Hawks' tie. When a mad dog ran amok in the school, it was Mr. Maurice who herded the boys into the gym and Mr. Eric, who shot the dog. I cannot remember much of Mr. Maurice's pedantic speech, but if games had to be cancelled due to rain, he would announce that instead there would be "kinematographic entertainments in the gymnasium". And I learned from him never to speak of 'the larger half'. "One half cannot be larger than the other!". At lessons I continued to underachieve, although I do remember a unique occasion, when I received some unexpected praise from Mr. Maurice in a Latin lesson. He asked the class for English words that were derived from the Latin, 'anulus', meaning a ring. I asked if 'annual' could be a derivation, since a year was a sort of circle. Mr Maurice looked at me in surprise, as if that reply should have come from someone else and said "intelligent answer". I do not know what his reaction would have been, if I had suggested a possible derivation to be the word 'anus'.

I remember also Mr. Green, a natural teacher, who, I learned later, had won the Military Cross in the horrors of the Trenches in the First World War. How cushy the life of his generally spoiled pupils must have seemed by comparison. I remember too a Dutch geography master, Mr. Ruygrok for one remark, which stayed with me. I don't mean he taught us Dutch geography; I mean he was Dutch andtaught us geography. He said that the English spelled the word 'I' as a capital letter, because we were so full of our own importance. Funny how these random memories stay with one.

At prep school we were all known by our surnames. Only closest friends were trusted with our first names. Nowadays it is the reverse. The surname seems to be a bit of a secret:
"My wife is not in at the moment. May I ask who's calling?"
"It's Sharon."
You feel you are being nosey, if you dare to ask which particular Sharon is calling. Perhaps the surname has become as guarded a secret as the prep-school boy's first name used to be. The surname needs to be re-invented. For the time being I might have to be satisfied with labelling the caller as 'Sharon from Accounts'.

On the subject of surnames, when my mother had to move to a private retirement home due to lack of mobility, the staff all immediately addressed her by her first name, Olive. She was not happy with this intimacy and politely asked to be called 'Mrs. Ordish'. When it came to her birthday, a special cake was iced and the staff led the singing of 'Happy Birthday' for the occasion, the last line of the song being, "Happy Birthday, Mrs. Ordish, Happy Birthday to you."

GRUMP, BARKING DOGS

As I write this, a nearby dog is barking and barking and barking. If, instead of being a barking dog, it was a person talking, they could have recited at least the whole of 'Gray's Elegy' by now. Dogs are capable of remarkable achievements such as sniffing out drugs or explosives and digging their owners out of snowdrifts. They do things that apparently display a remarkable level of intelligence, but they never seem to notice that barking doesn't get them anywhere. Like Edinburgh's famous Greyfriars Bobby, who reputedly sat on his dead master's grave for fourteen years, they just don't know when to stop.I wonder if Greyfriars Bobby was a barker? – probably not, or the gravediggers would surely have secretly interred him on a dark night.

This dog across the road here barks several thousand times a day. I worked it out. It does about fifty barks a minute and usually barks for around twenty minutes at a stretch. That gives it an hourly barking rate of three thousand b.p.h. It seems to bark about half the time, but maybe I am exaggerating. Let us assume it barks only a third of the time. Allowing it (and me) eight hours sleep at night, we can estimate that it barks sixteen thousand times a day. Why don't dogs get sore throats? I have never heard of vets getting call-outs from owners worried that their pet has got laryngitis?

As an experiment I tried doing some sustained barking myself and after just a couple of minutes I could already feel the strain on my vocal chords. My research also set the dog across the road off on another barking session. I stopped. The dog scross the road didn't stop, but it did did cause another dog a bit further away to start barking in response. Then the two of them started the 'I'm not going to stop barking until you do' competition.

A few years ago a former BBC colleague, Phil Bishop, made the local news by shooting dead a neighbour's barking dog. He was prosecuted by the owner, and was given a conditional discharge, having to pay a sixty pound fine and to buy his neighbours a new dog. I wonder if the new dog was a barker. If not, I'd say it was worth every penny, but then, as far as I'm concerned, I would not have had the nerve (nor the shotgun).

3.

FAMILY

My mother was a keen genealogist and created a beautiful family album. She was keen to trace any possible aristocratic ancestry and may have allowed her romantic fancies to carry her away in that department. The calculable ancestry was probably more interesting anyway. Her paternal great-grandfather and great-great-grandfather, both called Stephen Harvey-James, had been proprietors of Botallack tin and copper mine in the extreme west of Cornwall. Their story has the makings of a family saga with good times and bad times as the prices of copper and tin rose and fell. It is said that the author , Winston Graham, got his inspiration for his Poldark novels from Botallack and when the BBC filmed the first series, the exterior of the mine was used as a location for much of the filming. My great-great-grandfather's house, Botallack House, was used as Poldark's home in the filming. Co-incidentally, a great friend from university and my daughter's godfather, Ralph Bates was cast as the wicked Warleggan in the BBC's first 'Poldark' series.

The social progress of the Harvey-James family can be seen in the schools that succeding Stephen Harvey-James's attended The first went (probably) to Penzance Grammar School, his son, the second Stephen Harvey-James went to Shrewsbury (what a journey that must have been in 1862). His son, my grandfather, went to Eton. The Shrewsbury man, my great-grandfather, became a distinguished member of the government of India, serving as the Law Secretary on the Viceregal Council, a post which carried an automatic knighthood, but he died young and suddenly, leaving my great-grandmother rather piqued at not being Lady Harvey-James. The world would not be anything like as overcrowded as it is, if everyone bred as slowly as my family does. My grandfather was born in 1875. My daughter's grandfather was born eighty-two years before she was and so on.

In discussions about global warming the size of the world's population never seems to get mentioned. Is it too a delicate matter? Might we find ourselves offending those religions, which encourage their followers to breed, in order to increase the numbers of devotees. There are over three times as many people helping to warm the globe now as there were when I was born and they would all like to have cars.

Back to the ancestors. My mother's mother's family was a bit more solidly upper middle class. My great-grandfather Milner was a colonel in the Royal Irish Regiment and on retirement became a military coach, helping to get borderline applicants through the Sandhurst entrance exam, including the Earl of Athlone, one of the denser members of the Royal Family. A great-great-grandfather was called Edward Strathearn Kent Butler, the first three names being those of his godfather, the Duke of Kent, father of Queen Victoria. The family enjoyed the rumour that Colonel Butler was more than just a godson to the Duke, although Kent was not as renowned for the number of illegitimate children as his brothers were, particularly 'Prinnie', the Prince Regent. Colonel Butler's father was stationed in Halifax, Nova Scotia, where the Duke of Kent was 'Commander-in-chief of British Forcesin the Maritime Provinces of North America', so who knows?

I have less information on my father's ancestry. His grandfather had a hat factory in Luton and was mayor of that town in 1905. Luton town's football eleven are still known as 'the Hatters', although sadly straw hats went out of fashion a long time ago. Boaters are no longer obligatory even at Tonbridge School. My father's cousin Geoffrey, married into money sufficiently to allow his son to be that blast from the past, a gentleman of leisure. Mark Ordish was not idle, though. For example, he built himself an aeroplane, in which he flew.

FAMILY

My paternal grandmother's father was Edward Edmonds and is recorded as having been a 'theatrical producer'. So there is another stage connection. Googling has not found me any more information on him. A dodgy lot, theatre people, though.

4.

I.Q.

In the early days of working with Jimmy Savile, he would sometimes counter my suggestions with the words, "My Mensa logic tells me differently" At the age of thirty- six, without telling anyone, I therefore took the Mensa I.Q. test. I imagine most people do that secretly. Reckoning myself to be average to thick, my score amazed me. I received this letter from Mensa:

"Your score puts your I.Q. in the top one per cent of the population." Typically an IQ of that level might earn you a First at Oxford or Cambridge.

So, why did I not shine at school? I think I know why: I was a lazy dreamer. Or maybe I.Q. tests don't prove anything. Their value is pooh-poohed by a lot of people (or is that just the other ninety-nine per cent of the population?) It may be that your score in an IQ test only illustrates your ability at doing IQ tests. Anyway, there I was, a member of Mensa and my I.Q. seemed to have survived sixteen years of heavy drinking and smoking.

Is 'underachiever' another one of those recently-devised labels like dyslexia or 'discalculia' (difficulty with mathematics)? It would certainly have appealed to me as an explanation for my relative lack of success in life. My teachers called me 'lazy', but let's not say 'lazy'. Can't we find another word? I know: I was an underachiever, That sounds much better. Was I bad at maths or did I suffer from dyscalculia? I do know that in my first year at university I achieved the equivalent of a 'first' in my economics statistics paper, so it looks as if I am not eligible for the 'dyscalculia' label. I have three times come second in the British Mensa Scrabble championship, so I fear that knocks dyslexia on the head as well. I may have to

I.Q.

fall back on 'lazy'. No, let's give it a more scientific-sounding name. How about 'can'tbiarstia'?

To get to school aged eight, I rode my bicycle to Yalding station and then took the train to Paddock Wood, where I changed for a train to Tonbridge station. From there I would take a bus to Yardley Park Road, walking the rest of the way to my prep school, Yardley Court. Travel-wise I was perhaps an over-achiever. How did I pass my time during my travels? Did I do my homework? Did I achieve? No, I day-dreamed. In my life I do not think I ever had any driving ambition. I never cultivated powerful people, but I did have lots of fun.

Once home and after tea, I was allowed to listen to 'Dick Barton, Special Agent' on the BBC's Light Programme at 6.15. Only fifteen years later I would be producing a show that went out at 6.15 on the B.B.C. Light Programme. One episode of 'Dick Barton' became family folklore. Dick was in the office of a renowned criminologist. Let's call him Professor Smith. The professor was demonstrating to Barton some of the ingenious devices used by Barton's arch enemy, known as 'the Vulture'. Barton was invited to sit in a special chair, which had been somehow retrieved from the Vulture's lair. As soon as he sat down, some sort of clamp trapped Dick Barton in the chair, rendering him unable to move.

"Pretty impressive, Professor Smith," murmured Dick Barton, "It's a good thing you are not the Vulture!"

"That's just the point, Mr Barton," replied the professor, "I AM the Vulture!".

Cue disc, 'The Devil's Gallop'. Dum, diddle um, diddle um, diddle um.

Cue presentation voice: "How will Dick escape the Vulture's clutches? Tune in tomorrow to hear the next episode of 'Dick Barton, Special Agent!"

Time to do my prep. Well, I suppose I could always do it on the train tomorrow morning. Can'tbearstia had set in.

My father's work for I.C.I. sometimes took him to the U.S.A.. He would travel there by liner, spending five days at sea each way. He always took his dinner jacket. Life on board musthave been fairly luxurious compared with the misery of air travel today. He would bring back wonderful American luxuries to us in Austerity Britain. For me he brought an electric train set, a toy which was more or less unobtainable in the United Kingdom then. Being very ingenious, he was even able to manufacture a switching railway points system for me by cutting and soldering pieces of regular track together.

He also brought gramaphone records from the USA. There was an album of the musical 'Annie Get Your Gun', which really was an album, five or six 78 r.p.m. discs each with its own slot in between two hard covers. We played these records endlessly without fully understanding the words. The lyrics of 'You Can't Get a Man with a Gun' confused me.

"A Tom, Dick or Harry will build a house for Carrie, when the preacher has made them one."

If the preacher had already made a house for them, I wondered why would Tom, Dick or Harry want another one? If we sang some of these words at our Kindergarten, they might have caused Miss Paffard, our headmistress. to raise her eyebrows.

"She would hide behind a tree, doin' a what comes naturallee!"

My maternal grandfather, Arthur Harvey-James, whom I never knew, was one of the thousands of officers needlessly killed in the tragedy that was the First World War. The Eton College war memorial bears his name along with one thousand, one hundred and fifty six others. Next to his name is that of Basil Harvey-James, his only son, who was killed in the Second World War. My mother suffered the loss of both her father and her only brother in those conflicts. Eton College raised a massive War Memorial Fund, which offered free education at the school to the sons of those killed in the 'Great War'. Basil went to Eton free of charge.

I.Q.

I was my grandfather's only grandson and my uncle Basil left no offspring. My parents enquired of the Eton War Memorial Fund whether I might be eligible for fee relief. The reply came that, yes, I would be. I could not receive a free education at the school, as my uncle had done, but my fees could be reduced. My parents put my name down for this bursary. They thought that, by doing so, they had also put my name down for the school, but it turned out that that was not the case. I took the Common Entrance exam for Eton, but was warned that a place at the school was provisional on an insufficient number of entered boys reaching the required standard in the exam. One morning at 'Prayers' my prep-school headmaster, Mr. Maurice announced, "Ordish has passed for Eton, but the College has been unable to offer him a place. His Common Entrance papers will be therefore be passed on to Tonbridge School." But he warned, "Tonbridge School requires a higher mark than that accepted at Eton. So he will not necessarily pass for Tonbridge." I think Mr Maurice had a low opinion of Eton, not middle class enough, perhaps. Eton then had a surprisingly low academic standard at entrance level. Today their Common Entrance requirement level would be at least as high as Tonbridge's.

In my last school holiday before Tonbridge I was sent to Paris with the hope of improving my French. I stayed in the flat of a friend of my parents, Mademoiselle Deguillard, who was out at work from eight o'clock in the morning. She came back for lunch and then was away again in the afternoon. There I was on my own, aged thirteen, mastering the Paris Metro and touring around the city. Would that sort of thing happen today? I somehow think not. One of my joys was the discovery of the croissant. For my journey back to England I packed one into my bag. I had decided not to eat it until I was back in England. I travelled by train and ship, Paris-Dieppe-Newhaven-London. The boat train, as it was called in those days, had fairly old-fashioned carriages even by the standards of the 1950s. You opened a window by pulling on a leather strap, which could be hooked on a button to secure it in a half-open position. As the train pulled out of Newhaven Harbour, I opened the paper bag containing my precious croissant. There followed a snowstorm of croissant crumbs, as they were sucked out of the open train window. There must have been but a mouthful of the more doughy centre left for me to eat, but all my crumbs of comfort were out of the window. In a few weeks' time I was to start life at a public school.

5.

TONBRIDGE

So, Tonbridge School it was to be. For all the wrong, snobbish reasons I had longed to go to Eton. Being an Old Etonian still carries a special cachet but I do not know if I would have been happy there. I might have been mocked for my parents' relative lack of funds. Even at Tonbridge I felt ashamed of the strange old car that I would arrive in on the first day of term. It was a 1936 Lanchester 18 saloon, a brilliant vehicle, technically way ahead of its time in design but not like other parents' cars. It had a 'fluid flywheel' transmission, which meant the driver could pre-select a gear-change, simply kicking the clutch, when the change was required. It was similar to the system in a modern automatic car, when the driver selects 'manual'. The car had a large interior with a sun roof, tip-up spare seats in the back and tasselled handles for the rear passengers to grab on to as the car rounded a corner. The sun-roof did leak on rainy days, but we kept a plastic cup in the back to catch the drips. In truth, it was an altogether superior vehicle to the Morris Oxfords and Wolseleys that parked in the Judde House drive on 'exeat' days. I am now ashamed of having been ashamed.

When I wrote 'Old Etonians' just now, my computer's spell check asked, 'Did you mean Old Estonians?' That conjures up a very different picture. On the subject of Eton, In 1991 I wrote to an old school friend, Chris Stuart-Clark, who taught there. I told him that my grandfather and uncle were both on the shockingly long 'roll of honour', listing all the Old Etonians killed in the First and Second World Wars. I asked him if it might be possible for Susie, my wife, Lulu, our daughter and me to go to the school chapel service on Remembrance Day. Chris fixed it for me! He tucked us into a staff pew, from where we had a marvellous view of that elegant fifteenth century building. The excellent choir and lusty singing of the boys brought back memories of Tonbridge. After the service Chris had arranged for us to have drinks with the headmaster. Lulu asked the headmaster if it might be possible for a girl to go to Eton (and maybe benefit from the bursary offered me). He replied charmingly and mysteriously, saying, "It has been done".

It was shocking to look at the huge number of names on the 'Roll of Honour'. Hundreds of young men, needlessly cut down in their prime, some just eighteen or nineteen years old, nearly all officers, even at that age. My grandfather, aged forty two, was one of the oldest. The number of officers on the roll of honour shows how much the class system prevailed then, but it was said that an officer was more likely to be killed than the other ranks.

In my first few terms at Tonbridge School, some foodstuffs were still rationed, butter and sugar for example. Each boy had his own butter jar and sugar jar. We received two ounces of butter a week and four ounces of sugar. In the summer terms it was best to get through the butter fairly quickly, before the sun's rays through the glass of the jar made the butter go off, or that was my excuse, anyway. It is interesting to note that. as soon as butter was no longer rationed, we dispensed with the personal jars and got only margarine. I suppose it was because butter was no longer considered an essential. The school did not have a central dining hall, the boys eating their meals in the houses, about fifty boys to a house. That made for better food. I remember that breakfast, so important to a growing lad, would sometimes be just a fried egg and sometimes just bacon. I longed to have bacon AND egg and one morning abstained from my bacon, carefully wrapping it in a clean handkerchief. The following morning was an egg day. At breakfast I carefully unwrapped yesterday's bacon from the handkerchief and laid it alongside the egg. The bacon was a bit fluffy, but I had achieved my goal. I imagine I did that only once. Rather silly!

GRUMP - SHOWERS

The showers at school were basic and communal. One had to get used to public nudity, but, since we were not allowed even to close our lavatory doors, that seemed a minor deprivation. At least in the school showers there was somewhere to put the soap.

I enjoy soaking in a big, warm bath, but many people only ever take showers. How do they manage to wash their feet? Maybe they don't. In the bath, after my feet have soaked in the warm water for a minute or two, I like to exfoliate any dead skin from them, rendering them smooth and very clean. Trying to clean my feet in the shower is almost impossible. I lean against one wall, stand on one leg and, if there is anything to hold, hold on with one hand. I raise one foot and then drop the soap. I repeat the process, until I manage to get some soap on to the foot. But my feet have not been soaked; they are not ready for exfoliation. I put the soapy foot on the floor. It is slippery and I am in danger of falling over. I decide not to clean my feet. I'll wait until my next bath. With difficulty I retrieve the soap from the floor, but there is nowhere to put it. The smartest modern showers have smooth, marble walls. The only thing to hold on to is usually the hot water pipe, which is too hot to hold. If you have passed the exams necessary to operate the shower's controls, you may be able to vary the flow and temperature of the water. I have never been able to do that yet, well, certainly not on the first use any shower that I have ever entered. I usually exit the shower, covered in soap, wet, unclean, shivering or scalded and vowing to take a bath at the first opportunity.

6.

SCHOOL

Silliness at school reared its head again in a rather clever practical joke we played on one boy, Stephen Unwin. He was the sort of person you played practical jokes on, an indefinable quality. I hope what we did was just funny and not cruel. One of the latest bits of kit at that time was the tape recorder. Graham Roffey had a top of the range Grundig. At a certain stage of seniority each boy in the house would get a study of his own. They were tiny rooms with just space for a built-in desk, a chair and a small cupboard. Any electrical items had to be plugged into the light socket above the desk. There would sometimes be four or five extensions dangling from the cable above the light bulb. We pre-recorded our surprise for Unwin, when we knew he was out. Placing the tape recorder in his little cupboard, we somehow attached its cable to the light socket. It was dark, when Unwin returned to his study. He switched on the light, thereby also activating the tape recorder. We had allowed a few seconds of silence to let the machine warm up. We were listening outside the door, when our pre-recorded message began. Unwin heard a violent thumping coming from inside his tiny cupboard. "Help, help! Let me out!" cried a voice. "Let me out!" Unwin rose from his chair and stared, dumbfounded, at the cupboard, not daring to open it. It was at that that point that we entered his study and explained the situation. I am glad to say that he laughed as well.

Things like that happened to Stephen Unwin. During G.C.E.s and A-Levels, boys not taking a particular exam at any time, were expected to revise in a huge room, which I believe had served as the classroom for the entire school hundreds of years ago. We sat at desks, which could be folded and stacked to save space. Unwin fell asleep during one of these revision periods. He slumped forward on to his desk, somehow causing it to fold and hit the floor with Unwin on top of it. In what had been a deathly silence, it caused a tremendous crash. The senior classics master, a Mr. Howarth, was invigilating the revision and remarked drily, "These desks are designed to prevent somnia." I do not know if there is such a word as 'somnia', but we all knew what Mr. Howarth meant.

Tonbridge was more or less solidly a middle-class establishment. An exception was Murray de Vere Beauclerk, who was a direct descendant of King Charles the Second and Nell Gwynn. He is now the fourteenth Duke of St Albans. I remember sharing a couple of de Reszke cigarettes with him in the hop-field opposite Judde House. No Woodbines for Murray. I have just Googled that brand name and seen that de Reszke described their brand as 'the aristocrat of cigarettes'. How appropriate. On seeing a letter from William Hill addressed to Murray, our housemaster intercepted it and asked Murray,

"Have we been having a little flutter on the gee-gees, Beauclerk?"

"Oh no, sir," replied Murray but I think he had. The family had a great horseracing tradition.

Occasionally there would be concerts in 'Big School', which was, as its name implies, the largest assembly room. One evening a reedy tenor gave a concert there, which included Schubert Lieder and some of those 'tidied-up' folk songs that don't sound folksy at all, 'Sweet Lass of Richmond Hill', etc. The singer announced his final offering thus:

"And now, Mr. Headmaster, with your permission, I should like to change the tone of the proceedings and sing a Negro spiritual,"

What would we say nowadays? Just 'a spiritual', I suppose. The song he announced had one of those titles that would today be considered at best patronising. Something like, "All God's Chillum Sho' am Sleepin' in de Middle ob de Ribber." How times have changed.

I did a bit of singing myself. There was 'Down by the Ash Grove' in an inter-house harmony singing competition, while by contrast

I was the vocalist in the school jazz band. We rehearsed a lot and performed very seldom. As part of a school concert I sang 'Mama Don't Allow no Jazz-band Playin' in Here', which gave each instrument, trombone, clarinet and trumpet a 'break' after which I did impersonations of some of the staff. Not long after that performance we had a 'divinity' class with the school Chaplain, Mr Gripper (really). We read some of that strange passage from Ezekiel – I had to look it up to get the words right: "*The hand of the Lord carried me out in the spirit of the Lord and set me down in the midst of the valley, which was full of bones.... Prophesy upon these bones and say unto them, O ye dry bones, hear the word of the Lord*". Knowing perhaps that I had sung the song, "Dem Bones gonna Walk Around" with the jazz band, the chaplain interrupted the reading to address me, "These words may be familiar to you, Ordish."

One of my school subjects was German, which I did well enough in to sit my 'O' level a year early. That was partly due to the fact that I had done an exchange with a German boy of my age, Rüdiger Barbrock, or 'Bludiger Rüdiger' as he came to be known. When I stayed with his family near Essen, it was only ten years after the war and the terrible bombing that the Ruhrgebiet had suffered was still evident, despite the great amount of reconstruction that had gone on. I felt on some of our trips, as if I was being taken to see the scenes of my war crimes, such as the severely damaged Cologne Cathedral. We also visited Lake Möhne, which in the war had been successfully breached by the bouncing bombs, dropped by Guy Gibson and the team known as the 'Dam Busters'. I disclaimed any responsibility, but remembered that our housemaster, Alfred Foster, though not aircrew himself, had been part of that operation. Mr. Foster dismissed Gibson as a dreadful man, adding, "and as for that dog....".

Gibson's black Labrador was called the now unspeakable N-word. In later television transmissions of the famous Dam Busters' film, they managed to dub the dog's name as 'Digger'. I am not sure about that name, though. It may have offended some Australians? You have to be so careful nowadays.

During my exchange stay in the Ruhrgebiet, my hosts often said things I did not fully understand, but let them go, rather than constantly seek translations. One question, to which I should not have answered 'Ja', complicated things a bit. With the family I set off in the car, vaguely wondering where we were going. A bomb site, perhaps. We travelled on and on, out of the suburbs of Essen onward and up into the Harz mountains. The question I had replied 'Ja' to turned out to be. "Have you packed your suitcase for the weekend in our holiday cottage?" Of course, I hadn't.

7.

SPORT AT SCHOOL

Like many public schools, Tonbridge laid great importance on sport. If you were not good at games, you were a nobody. I was a nobody. In my negative way, instead of trying to improve, I did not try at all. On more than one occasion I managed to play a game of what we then called 'rugger' without ever touching the ball and I learned that, if I took a 'deep field' position in cricket, I could with luck merge into the background and would not have to change my position at the end of an over. My time at the crease was mercifully short, since I was usually out first ball. Luckily for me, we were obliged to play cricket only for our first summer term. The following summer I was able to join the Boat Club. Not having a 'ball eye' did not matter in rowing and I really rather enjoyed it. The river Medway in Tonbridge was too narrow for eight-man boats, so we rowed fours. In spite of being fairly weedy, I managed in my last summer to be selected for the school Third Four. We competed in the Gravesend Regatta, where we won a cup, beating a team of policemen in the final. When learning to row on a 'sliding seat', if you position yourself badly, it is easy to develop sores on your bottom. If that was the case, Mrs Debrowski, our house matron, would rub cream into the tender area of the buttocks. This was alarmingly pleasant for a growing lad. I was never sure if she was aware of the effect her massage was having on the average young oarsman. On reflection, I think she probably was.

I continued to row at Trinity College, Dublin. The eight that I was a member of contained a lot of posh boys, three Old Etonians and a coxswain from Shrewsbury. Eton, I noticed, would no longer automatically get you into Oxford or Cambridge. One of the many Etonians at Trinity was Hamish Riley-Smith, who went on to become a renowned dealer in extremely rare books. At Trinity he was known as Hamish Really-Smooth.

SPORT AT SCHOOL

The only other school sport, at which I could claim any prowess was athletics, another pursuit that required no skill with a ball. I could run quite fast for a short time and managed to squeeze into the junior athletics squad as the fourth fastest boy in the four man relay team. I tried to play squash, asking a friend to coach me. I can still remember the humiliation of being unable to serve the ball amid jeers from the viewing gallery, as with swipe after swipe, the ball continued to bounce mockingly on the wooden floor. Later in life, when I was at the B.B.C., I played a bit of squash, only ever playing against women, which was delightful in two ways. I had more of a chance of winning and I love the company of women. By then I must have learned how to serve a squash ball. It kept me in touch with my masculine side.

The emphasis of sport at school and the ignominy of being bad at it has tended to make me anti-sport in later life. A particular irritation is sport commentary on television.

The silent movies preceded talkies by twenty or thirty years. Pictures arrived before sound. In broadcasting it was the other way round. Radio preceded television. Before there was TV, radio would sometimes cover sporting events. Wimbledon would not have made much sense, if all you could hear was the whacking of tennis balls and the occasional cries of, "Well played, sir," A commentator was essential to tell listeners what was going on. When television came along, without thinking about it very much, the BBC and others continued to employ commentators. But are they necessary? Do we need someone to tell us what we can already see? People pay hundreds, if not thousands of pounds, for a seat at Wimbledon or the Cup Final. They do not get a commentary. Maybe they pay all that money just to escape what essentially has to be waffle, since we can see that a goal has been scored or that that a double fault has just been served.

Talking of tennis, who started this fist-shaking by tennis players, who have just played a winning shot? It looks angry and most unsportsmanlike. When played in slow motion, as it frequently is, it looks vaguely (or not very vaguely) obscene, as if a comment was being passed on the ability of one's opponent.

8.

SCHOOL CORPS

The school corps, the Combined Cadet Force, was compulsory and the whole school would appear in chapel on Monday mornings wearing army or air force uniform. In the fifties all the boys at school were expecting to do National Service. A good grounding in military things gave you a better chance of getting a commission during your call-up and having a more interesting time as an officer for those two years.

The highlights of the 'Corps' year were 'field days' once a term, a week of 'camp' in the summer holidays and an annual General's inspection. There was an old boy of the school with the wonderful pre-Norman name of Edmond Ironside, who came to inspect the corps in my first term at Tonbridge. He had been a brigadier in the First World War and seemed incredibly old to us boys. He was then Field Marshal Lord Ironside. Standing next to the headmaster, he addressed the whole school.

"When I came to this school all those years ago," he began, "we were like young porcupines with our pricks sticking out."

It says something for the discipline of the school that the ensuing sniggers were only just audible. My friend, Tim, says that Ironside was under the impression that he was addressing the pupils of Stowe. I do not remember that bit. Was he senile? I have just looked up the field marshal's dates and noticed that at the time he was six years younger than I am now. Oh dear!

For my expected National Service I wanted to try for the Royal Air Force, where it was harder to get a commission, but offered the possibility of an exciting life as a pilot. So I chose to go into what was called the Air Section of the corps. Going for a week to an R.A.F. station in the summer holidays was part of the training. It certainly showed me how dull national service as an 'Aircraftsman Two' in the RAF could be. I remember observing one national serviceman, who was mopping a linoleum floor. He had filled a red 'fire' bucket with soapy water, into which from time to time he dismally dipped his mop, but, while his back was turned, someone else removed the fire bucket, maybe in order to mop another floor. The A.C.2 turned round to refresh his mop and discovered that his 'fire' bucket had disappeared. He expressed his dissatisfaction in the most elaborate piece of swearing I have ever heard:

"Some fucking fucker's fucked me fucking fucker bucket!"

I remember a night exercise, where we cadets had to attempt to enter the airfield and elude the RAF police. Spotting some ill-trained teenagers, a dog handler shone his torch in our direction and shouted, "Halt, or I shall release my dog!" we continued to inch forward in the darkness The dog handler repeated his warning, "Halt, or I shall release my dog!" We continued to creep forwards. Finally in exasperation, the handler shouted,

"If I didn't know who you were, I'd release my dog!"

We slept in bunk beds in grim Nissen huts. By contrast on another occasion, when the school corps had been inspected by a visiting Air Marshal, he made an offer to the school. Anyone who was interested in a career in the R.A.F. could apply to spend a week in the officers' mess of a fighter station and the week would include flights in a two-seater 'Meteor' jet fighter. I applied and was accepted for a visit. Three of us went to R.A.F. West Malling. We were not in uniform, since we could not stay in the officers mess in lowly aircraftsmen's outfits, but we were told we had to wear hats. I had to buy a trilby for the occasion. West Malling was a thrilling experience. I remember being strapped into a two-seater 'Meteor' trainer for a daytime flight. The pilot flew low over the sea at Brighton and said to me over the intercom: "Watch that man showing off on the edge of his boat." He executed a swift turn and dived alarmingly low over the water. We went round again and could see that the show-off was now in the sea.

SCHOOL CORPS

"Would you like me to do a barrel roll?", the pilot asked me. The thought was scary, but how could I say 'No'? Google describes a barrel-roll thus: 'an aerobatic manoeuvre in which an aircraft follows a single turn of a spiral while rolling once about its longitudinal axis'. It's not something you would want to do in an airliner. Gulp. Even more glamorous was to sit in the navigator's seat of the two-seater night-fighter for a night flight.

Back at school at one point I was one of two sergeants in the air cadet corps. The other sergeant, Ronald Wilson, was to become Air Chief Marshal Sir 'Sandy' Wilson, K.C.B., A.F.C. He would almost certainly have been the last ever to hold the top rank in the force, Marshal of the Royal Air Force, a rank which no longer exists except for Royalty. The reason Sandy did not reach that status was due to a scandal concerning overspending on furnishings for his official residence. Who was to blame is not clear. Was he a scapegoat? Was it his over-ambitious wife's fault, as a gossip whispered to me at an old boys' reunion?

My job in my last term in the Air Section put me in that rare category, 'excused boots', normally reserved for men with trench foot. That was because I was in charge of a rudimentary flight simulator, the Link Trainer, which was housed in an air-conditioned hut, where dust was the enemy. The floor had to be kept immaculately clean to enable the delicate machinery to do its job of simulating flight and recording the 'journey' the aircraft had taken. A red inked nib traced the trainer's virtual trip on a glass sheet laid on top of a local map. It was even possible to go into a spin and 'crash'. Great fun!

The other toy in the Air Section was not so delicate, a very primitive glider, the Eton Mark Six. The pilot had control of an anchor, pinning the craft to the ground, while six boys on each side of the aircraft walked forwards, pulling two large elasticated ropes. The further the boys walked with the ropes, the further the glider would travel on release. It was a sort of game of 'chicken' as to when the pilot would order the pullers to halt and release his anchor. We launched a boy called Ross, who must have lost his nerve on take-off. He steered the glider a few feet forwards into the air and then suddenly pushed the rudder hard over to the left, causing the glider to loop round, until was it was facing in the opposite direction, which meant Ross was heading directly at a line of hurdles laid out in preparation for an athletics match. Luckily, he was flying in the direction that the hurdlers would take, which meant the glider knocked the hurdles over fairly easily. Ross was unhurt, but the glider was out of action until further notice.

9.

ACTING

If I shone in anything at school, it might have been acting. For better or worse there are quite a few actors in my ancestry. My maternal grandfather, Arthur Harvey-James, went out to India as a journalist on 'The Times of India', but, while in India was persuaded to join a touring company of players and his career thereafter was as an actor. His wife to be, my maternal grandmother, also from a respectable middle class family, likewise went on the stage. They met in the theatre and had enough success on the stage to keep body and soul together, but must always have been dogged by the actor's eternal worry, "Where is the next job going to come from?" My paternal grandmother's father also had theatrical connections. Edward Edmonds was an actor manager. According to what my grandmother told me many years ago, he was at one time manager of the Lyceum Theatre, London, but I have not been able to confirm that with a 'Google' search.

A bit of a challenge for a sixteen year old boy at an all boys school was taking the part of Prospero in Shakespeare's 'The Tempest', one of the longest parts in the Complete Works. I did manage to learn the lines. How well I spoke them was another matter. There was a scene, in which Prospero conjures up the nymphs, Iris, Juno and Ceres to perform in a 'masque', celebrating the betrothal of Miranda and Fernando. The problem was that three boys, all known to the audience, wafting about the stage in flimsy, gauze costumes as nymphs was too much for that butch, athletic crowd. Poor old Prospero had to shout some of his lines over the jeers and catcalls.

Usually the boy who took the lead in the school play was made a member of a society founded by the headmaster and called the Athena Society, aimed at creating a sort of intellectual élite of the school. Unfortunately his opinion of my intellectual level must have been so low, that he called me to his study to apologise for NOT making me a member of the Athena Society. Since I was far from having any sporting 'colours', I had been rather hoping to wear the distinguished-looking Athena tie. Ah, well.

I only once heard Mr. Waddy, the headmaster, tell a joke, but it was one I rather liked. It was about a theological postgraduate student, who kept failing to obtain his doctorate of divinity. When he was asked what the title of his thesis was to be, he replied, "I've called it, 'Towards an Approach'".

I continued to be fairly idle in class, always trying to do just enough 'prep' to get away with it (you couldn't call it 'homework' there). But there were two masters, who for me were inspirational. Logie Bruce-Lockhart possessed everything needed to be a schoolboy hero: a Cambridge rugby and squash Blue, who also played rugby for Scotland, a wartime officer in the Household Cavalry and a brilliant teacher.* (Footnote: *He was one of the first British soldiers to enter the Bergen-Belsen concentration camp at its liberation*)

He taught us French in a wonderfully original way. I believe any kind of learning by rote is frowned on today, but his chants reminding us of French constructions and pronunciation have stayed with me to this day:

"Papa alla à la plage" (daddy went to the beach) I can still hear Logie's deep, bass voice resonating on the French 'g' of 'plage'.

"Le perroquet du Président est parti pour le Paradis." (the President's parrot has left for Paradise.)

"La pauvre bête, elle vit apparaître à la fenêtre les têtes de seize maîtres." (The poor beast, she saw the heads of sixteen masters appear at the window)

He also had us sing somewhat bawdy French songs. For example, 'Les Fraises et les Framboises'.

"...Les belles villageoises, nous ne les reverrons plus,

J'en ai choisi la plus belle et la plus jeune aussi,

Je l'ai montée à ma chambre, pour lui parler du pays."

(The beautiful village girls, we shall never see them again. I chose the most beautiful of them, who was also the youngest. I took her up to my room to talk to her about the countryside. It makes me think of Hamlet's 'country matters'.)

Not exactly politically correct, but that was 1957 for you.

There was another master, Richard Bradley, who rumbled me. "Ordish, you are cleverer than you pretend to be," he claimed. He was one of those inspired teachers and he took us for a class that was ideally suited to his talent. There was not a G.C.E. or 'A' Level to aim for. His class was pure education. Each week we had to write a 'journal' with topics of our own choice, which would then be a subject for group discussion. Mr. Bradley inspired me to want to go to university, although my scholastic record did not suggest I was suited to it. After cramming, struggles and unsurprising failures at Oxford and Cambridge, I was finally accepted by Trinity College, Dublin, a wonderful establishment, founded by Queen Elizabeth the First in 1592. Inevitably it was a Protestant foundation, creating a delicate situation in largely Catholic Ireland.

10.

GAP YEARS

Sometime between school and university three friends and I took an unreliable trip to Italy. Our vehicles were Tim Waterstone's 1936 Morris Tourer Convertible and Mark Denby's BMW Isetta. Don't think of BMWs as we know them now. The Isetta had a 250cc engine, three wheels and opened at the front. Its advantage was that it could do ninety miles to the gallon. Somehow we got to Venice and back, despite discovering at one point that a passport had fallen through the floor of Tim's car, where we had placed it 'safely' under the mat surrounding the pedals. Our journey home took us through a part of Germany. Tim stopped the car just as we were about to join an Autobahn. There were no motorways in Britain then. Tim turned to me and said, "You can drive this bit. Autobahn driving is easy." He was wrong, but once I had taken the wheel, there was no stopping until we got off the motorway again. If I remember rightly, I had not driven at all before that. I certainly did not have a licence. I kept pulling into the right too sharply after overtaking, causing lorry drivers to hoot and brake. Somehow we reached the safety of a minor road. We could so easily have finished up with a bent car and a police cell.

My father left I.C.I. in the sixties and started working for the United Nations Food and Agriculture Organisation, whose headquarters were in Rome. That meant we had a temporary flat in Rome. My sort-of girlfriend, Anthea, went at the same time to a finishing school in Rome run by a Contessa Bedini. The Bedinis were owners of the unique Anglo-Italian Babbington's Tea Rooms, just next to Rome's famous Spanish Steps. The family was totally bilingual and enjoyed literally translating the names of Italian people and places into English. Their Porto Santo Stefano villa was in St. Stephen's Port and their houseboy, Primo, was Primus.

Tim Waterstone came to stay a few days in the Rome flat. He and I hitch-hiked to Naples and discovered a foodstuff hitherto unknown to us. It was called Pizza. We slept one night on Anzio beach with no bedding. Amazing, what we could do at that age and amazing how wet the morning dew can be.

While waiting and hoping to go to university I got a teaching job at a local prep school, Aylesford House in Sandridge near St Albans. I note that the school no longer exists, so I feel free to say that it was more or less a dump. Life there was made tolerable by the fact that another young man, John Bridgen, was also hired to join the teaching staff at the same time as me. He was a brilliant musician, waiting to take up his place at King's College, Cambridge. We shared digs down in the village, not far from the pub, where in the evenings we would laugh ourselves silly about life at the school. There were two joint headmasters, Mr. Thompson and Mr. Lee, referred to privately as Laurel and Hardy, whom they did physically resemble. Mr Thompson was Oliver Hardy, very much the dominant partner, who lived in the best part of the old manor house that had become the school. I do not remember where poor Mr Lee lived. At morning assembly Mr. Thompson might say, "We have decided..", to which Mr. Lee might reply, "Have we?". "Yes, we have.", Mr Thompson would declare emphatically. John and I called Thompson 'fars major', in an imaginary Latin, *fars, fartis*, the Great Fart.

While I was teaching at Aylesford House, my elder sister, Jenny, got married. Tim Waterstone and I were to be ushers at her wedding. At the school I changed into my hired morning coat and ordered a taxi to take me to St Albans Cathedral, where the wedding was to take place. I waited and waited, but no taxi appeared. I stood in the road, looking conspicuous in my top hat and tails. I decided to try and thumb a lift. I had no luck from passing cars, but eventually a dustcart came along and stopped. The idea of picking up a stranded toff must have appealed to the driver. I made it to the cathedral. Maybe the driver was Alfred Doolittle. Talk about 'get me to the church on time'!

I taught, amongst other subjects, maths, which I enjoyed doing enormously. Maths teachers should not be good mathematicians. I was badly taught at prep school by the retired head of maths from Harrow school. Probably a brilliant mathematician, he could not understand how people could find the subject difficult. I remember him showing us how to use logarithm tables without explaining what logarithms were. I said to another boy after some difficult maths homework "Hey, I've discovered that, if you just do the sum without using the log tables, you still get the correct result." I thought I had made a great discovery. For my younger readers, that was like saying, "If you do the sum without using a calculator, you will still get the right answer." In maths lessons at Aylesford House I would occasionally be told, "Oh, at last I understand, sir!". Most rewarding.

For some reason I once had to referee a rugger match against another prep school. Having only the vaguest memory of the rules, I was alarmed to see the visiting school's sports master standing on the touchline, wearing an Oxford Blue's scarf. Fairly soon into the game an event occurred, for which I did not know the rule. I think it was a kick-off where the ball went right over the defending side's goal line, the ball being touched down by one of the defending team. I ordered a kick-off from the half-way line. There was a cry from the touchline, "I beg your pardon!". It was the Oxford Blue, "That should be from the twenty-five yard line!" he bellowed. "Oh yes, of course," I said, "Silly me!"

I still had another year to wait before my university place became available. The log jam was caused by the arrival of men, who had completed their two years' National Service and the younger men, like me, who would no longer be conscripted. I had had enough of Aylesford House and took a job at another country house converted into a prep school. It was St Leonard's Forest

School, a twentieth century mock Tudor mansion set in beautiful woodland near Horsham, Sussex. There was a desperately serious master there, a Mr Moll, who usually wore his Cambridge Hawks tie. I remember him fretting about the school's poor performance in cricket matches against other schools and I thought how ridiculous it was to be so concerned about these little boys' prowess on the playing field, but a few months later, when I had been put in charge of athletics, I heard myself expressing similar concerns about the boys' inability to do proper 'crouch' starts for a sprint.

I was walking round the beautiful school grounds with the headmaster one summer evening and he asked me if I could smell burning. I agreed that I could and we started searching high and low, trying to locate the source of the smell. Wherever we went, there was the same pungent aroma. Eventually we discovered that the smell was coming from the headmaster's jacket pocket, where a box of Swan Vestas was smouldering away in its limited oxygen supply. When he hastily threw the box away, it immediately exploded in the fresh air, but the jacket was saved.

11.

DUBLIN

In October, 1960, I started at Trinity College, Dublin. At first I felt a bit lonely in suburban digs run by a puritanical protestant woman. The other residents were mostly Ulstermen reading theology. It felt far removed from my Oxbridge fantasy, but I started to make friends on my economics and political science course and then discovered 'Players', the college dramatic group. I watched an impressive production of 'The Long and the Short and the Tall', a hit by Willis Hall, which in only the previous year had starred Peter O'Toole at London's Royal Court Theatre. My friend-to-be, David O'Clee was brilliant in it and seeing his performance made me enrol immediately to become a member of 'Players'.

In a rather blinkered way the then Roman Catholic Archbishop of Dublin forbade Irish Catholics from attending the college, although there were plenty of Catholics there from England, Scotland and Wales. In Dublin at that time, if there were nuns on a bus, they would cross themselves when their bus passed Trinity. I never was quite sure what that signified, a blessing for the infidels, perhaps. Trinity was much like one very large Oxford or Cambridge college with the trappings that pleased me: dining wearing our gowns in an ancient hall full of portraits of former alumni, a year or two in college rooms, shared with a fellow undergraduate and waited on by a college servant. I shared with a man called Dan Hearn, the opposite of me, a very keen Rugby player. His plan was to play Rugby for Trinity, which might enable him to do a post-graduate year at Oxford, taking a diploma for education there, which, he hoped would get him a teaching post at a top public school. He was extremely successful in his ambitions. He played for Trinity, went to Oxford, played for Oxford University and then got selected to play for England. What a triumph! If only he had stopped there. But in an unimportant game in Leicester, he mistimed a tackle and broke his neck. Although condemned to be a paraplegic for the rest of his life, his spirit kept him going and despite his handicap he taught successfully at Haileybury College for 35 years.

We were 'reading' Economics. We had only eight lectures a week but, surprisingly, two of them were consecutive and in the same lecture theatre. After an hour, Professor Ryan (economic theory) replaced Mr. Thornton (statistics). Professor Ryan entered the theatre and observed that Mr. Thornton's state-of-the-art Pitney Bowes calculating machine was still on the lectern. He looked at the device wryly and said. "I see that the previous lecturer has left his brains behind."

The father of one of my fellow undergraduates, David Ridley, was the agent to the enormously wealthy Duke of Westminster. Think of any street in London that has the words 'Eaton' or 'Grosvenor' in it and it will belong to the duke. Oh and there's Mayfair and Park Lane as well , where Grosvenor House is. And that's some of just their property in London. My friend David invited me to join the dowager Duchess's party for an outing to Aintree racecourse for the Grand National. I leapt at the opportunity, but was extremely short of funds at the end of that 'Hilary' term. To get to Chester I took the boat from Dublin to Holyhead in Anglesey and decided to hitch-hike from there. When I arrived with nothing but a back pack full of random clothes, David Ridley was a bit worried about what I should wear for the Grand National outing . He lent me a rather smart tweed suit for the occasion, but, since he was three or four inches shorter than me, we had a problem with the length of the trousers. I extended the braces to their maximum and, pushing my hands into the trouser pockets, was able to hide my socks. But you can't walk around with your hands in your pockets, when you are with a duchess, so the trousers tended to spring back upwards once more.

We drove in two or three Bentleys to the racecourse and had a luxurious picnic in some reserved spot before going to our grandstand box. When it came to the big race, I sneaked away on my own to make a bet, since I had so very little money. For no good reason I put four shillings to win on a horse called Ayala. I could not hide my excitement, when Ayala won the race at sixty-six to one. The others in our party congratulated me on my luck and I did not like to say how small my bet had been. They probably thought I had laid a fiver. The next day was a striking contrast. I was hitchhiking again, but I did have an extra thirteen pounds in my pocket, which I reckon at today's prices would be about four hundred pounds.

At the end of my second year reading Economics, the opportunity arose for undergraduates to spend the summer vacation in the U.S.A. The flight would cost fifty pounds (about £1,500 at today's prices, but very cheap for air travel in 1962). In addition to that I bought a Greyhound Bus '$100 for 100 days' ticket and, by the time I completed my round trip, had travelled more than ten thousand miles on those buses. To start the immigration process I went to the American Embassy in London and applied for an immigrant's 'Green Card', nowadays a difficult thing to obtain, especially with the eight-year-old president they have there at the moment. In those days the United Kingdom did not reach its quota of permitted immigrants and the card was there for the asking. I declared that I was not a communist, promised to learn English and I was in. I borrowed the price of the air fare and bus ticket from my parents and swore to pay it back, when I returned from America (which I did). To do that, it was necessary for me to find a job for the first few weeks of my stay.

Through an agency I found employment as a waiter in a seaside hotel in Ogunquit, Maine. Nearly all the waiting staff were students. We served breakfast, cleared the dining room, laid tables for the evening meal and were free from midday until 5 p.m. With several people of my own age there, I was in good company. We were paid just one dollar a day. We added to that our tips, which were not pooled. I tried to sell myself with my Briddish accent.

I encountered a little language problem at the start. The 'hostess', who was in charge of us waiters, would ask me, "Are you all caught up, Roger?". I thought she meant, 'Have you caught up with the work you need to do?' and would reply, "Yes". I then discovered that 'caught up' meant 'busy'. Since she understood me to be saying that I had enough customers and my hands were full, she did not send customers to 'my' tables. Once that was sorted out, I started getting diners, most of whom left good tips.

"Hey, where are you from , waiter?"

"I'm from England and I am saving up to do a Greyhound bus tour of your wonderful country."

It worked fairly well and the additional dollars started to flow in. One rowdy crowd loved the accent and called me 'Mr. Christian', a reference to the recent movie, 'Mutiny on the Bounty', where Marlon Brando played Christian with a passable English tone. If boiled eggs were required at breakfast, we had to serve them peeled, which was usually done by the 'salad man', who must have had asbestos fingers. Two old biddies came down to breakfast one morning and when I served them their boiled eggs, one of them enquired, "Who peeled these eggs, waiter?"

"The salad man," I replied.

"Coloured man, did you say?", she shrieked in horror.

"No. Salad man."

She did not ask what colour the salad man was.

After about five weeks I reckoned I had accrued enough tips to finance my trip and I handed in my notice. Another student/waiter, Casey Kearse, was leaving the job at the same time. He had a car and proposed that I join him for a short trip through New Hampshire and northwards into Canada. It caused much amusement to our colleagues, when I told them that Casey and I were off to Niagara Falls. I did not get the joke, until it was explained that Niagara was renowned as a location for honeymoons and dirty weekends.

Casey was from Florida, but to my ears anyway had a southern drawl that I did not associate with that state. He was interested in where I came from and would ask things like, "Hey, Rodge boy, you got TV in England?" I told him we considered ourselves to have invented it, remembering the Scotsman from Bexhill-on-Sea, John Logie Baird.

When we crossed into Canada, he was surprised to see pictures of the Queen of England here and there. To save money we sometimes slept over night in the car, which was deeply uncomfortable, but that sort of thing is possible when you are twenty-one years old. Being twenty-one was important to my colleagues at the hotel in Maine It was the legal drinking age and, since some of the others were a year or two younger than me, it was I with my Green Card as proof of age, who would be sent to the bar to fetch the next round.

Back in the U.S.A. Casey dropped me off in Akron, Ohio on his way back to Florida and my next ten thousand miles would be travelled alone by bus. Using my precious dollars sparingly, I would sometimes sleep on a bus as it roared on through the night. The sheer size of the USA was amazing to one from our little island. I remember on one night falling asleep during a journey through the cornfields of Minnesota and waking up as the sun rose to discover that we were still travelling through the cornfields of Minnesota. I often struck up a conversation with whoever was sitting next to me and on more than one occasion was invited to get off the bus in their home town and spend a night as their guest. The generosity was overwhelming. Their religious sincerity struck me as being so different from the attitude of most of us cynical Europeans. I would not expect a 'grace' before a meal at all in England and, if there was one, it would be a mumbled affair, but in the Midwest it was even customised. "And God bless Roger, our visitor from England. May he be safe on his travels."

I had arranged to stay at the homes of two American students, who had been doing a year at TCD: Dee Manning in Denver,

Colorado and Jodi Saugstad in Hollywood, no less. Her father was a sound recordist with Warner Brothers and, as well as visiting the original Disneyland, I was able to go behind the scenes at Warner's and see some filming. My favourite Warner Brothers characters, Bugs Bunny, Sylvester and Tweetie Pie, were nowhere to be seen. I was running short of money and for the next three nights of my journey, which included a brief excursion into Mexico I slept on the bus. I remember crawling off the bus very early one morning in New Orleans and was thrilled to see a lamp-post bearing very familiar street names: Basin Street, Beale Street, Bourbon Street and South Rampart Street, all linked in my mind to famous Dixieland jazz tunes.

My next destination was Coral Gables, part of Miami, Florida. There lived the family of Grant Stockdale, a successful businessman and friend of President Kennedy, who had appointed Stockdale as the U.S. ambassador to Ireland, Grant's two daughters, Anne and Sally were friends with me at Trinity and invited me to stay in their Florida mansion. I arrived in the late afternoon after three or four nights spent sleeping on the bus and asked if the family would excuse me, if I went to bed straight away. When I awoke, it was twilight, I decided to wait until the sun rose before getting up. But, instead of getting lighter, it was getting darker. I had slept for twenty-four hours. Anne Stockdale later married English actor-comedian, John Bird. Her father was soon to be caught up in a complicated political scandal with mob connections and shortly after the president's assassination, either committed suicide or was pushed. It was never made clear.

After a couple of days I bussed back to New York, staying one night on the way in Baltimore with the Wurzburgers, a lovely couple, who had been my sponsors to immigrate to the USA. The Wurzburgers, friends of my parents, had amassed a fortune through 'real estate' and were great collectors of modern art. In England a couple of years earlier our family had accompanied them, when they visited the workshops of two British modern sculptors, Reg Butler and Henry Moore. Reg Butler had just won a major international competition with his piece entitled, 'Unknown Political Prisoner'.

These sculptors' works were generally beyond my comprehension, but the thing that secretly fascinated the family was the knowledge that Reg Butler had two wives, both apparently living in harmony with him at the same time. We had tea with the sculptor and his wives and tried not to look too nosey.

A shocking letter was waiting for me in Baltimore. I was instructed to present myself for a military 'physical' (medical). If I passed it, I would be eligible for call-up to go to the war in Vietnam. As a student returning to university, I was excused this alarming prospect, but now, whenever I go to the USA, my record comes up for scrutiny. It must say something like 'dissatisfied immigrant'. As the infantile President Trump would say, "Get him outa here!".

On the plane journey back to Dublin a rather hippy fellow undergraduate asked me what I had got up to in the U.S.A. I knew he regarded me as a retrograde young fogey and I told him that I had found an English pub in New York that served Young's Best Bitter and that I had stayed there all the time. He cast his eyes to the heavens.

Rather a mean practice at Trinity College, Dublin, was to hold the exams at the end of the summer vacations. Swots, I imagine, would spend the entire summer getting themselves ready for the October examination. Others would emigrate to the USA for three months. I scraped an overall pass mark for my exams, but one professor objected to the way I had worded one essay and marked it down to a level that would get me rusticated (sent down for a year). The question asked in the paper was "Why is a chicken more heavily subsidised by the state than a university professor?" The wording suggested to me that, while giving all the necessary facts in my answer, I could write it in a light-hearted way. I presented my essay as a newspaper article with headlines. The important fact I forgot was that Doctor Flynn had a humour quotient of zero. The light-hearted wording of my essay must have got up his nose.

My tutor, the delightful R.B.D. French, who looked after us in the university's dramatic society, 'The Players', came to my rescue and a compromise was reached. I could stay at the university, but would be demoted from my honours economics course to 'General Studies', for which I could only gain an 'ordinary' degree. At no time in my life since then did anyone ever ask me to show proof that I had a degree at all. I could have made the whole thing up.

12.

VIRGIN TRANSATLANTIC

Many of my male colleagues would boast of their sexual exploits. I was not really in a position to do the same, since I was a virgin. My girl friend was a beautiful, young Canadian dancer, Louise McCrow, whose father had come to Ireland to work for Telefis Eireann, which means Irish television. If you think English spelling is difficult, have a look at Irish spelling. One of my favourite lines in Richard Curtis's 'Vicar of Dibley' is when a young Irish woman introduces herself with a name that sounds like 'eefer'. "Is that spelt 'XQYJN?'", enquires another character. "Yes" replies the young woman.

Where was I? Ah, yes, Louise McCrow. In the most natural of circumstances we suddenly found that we were making love. I lost my virginity and Louise lost hers. Mother Nature decided we had chosen the wrong or right moment. Louise was pregnant. And that was the very first time for both of us! This was Catholic Ireland, whose celibate priesthood (ha, ha) insisted that their congregations reproduce at the greatest rate possible, in order to increase the size of the flock or, perhaps, to compensate for priesthood's celibacy. Contraception was banned and it was not possible to buy any kind of contraceptive device in the Republic. Anyway, it was too late. An abortion would have been illegal and therefore dangerous, leaving Louise and me not knowing what to do. As things turned out, a baby boy was born very prematurely some four or five months later and died after a few hours. The grim faced 'Sisters of Little Mercy' would of course not allow me to visit Louise in hospital and treated her horribly as punishment for her mortal sin. After that Louise and I drifted apart.

I was delighted to hear many years later from her father, then also working in BBC Television in London, that Louise was happily married and had two lovely children.

While I was at university, the level of unemployment in the United Kingdom was very low. That meant that vacation jobs were fairly easy to find. I was at one time or another a farmhand, tutor to an eleven year old viscount, a 'chain boy' during the building of the M1 motorway, a baker's roundsman, an office temp in Collet's communist bookshop, a gardener and, of course, a postman.

When applying for Christmas postal work, I filled in a form, which included the question, "Do you have any disabilities?" I wrote "I have broken my leg as the result of falling off a horse." So, what job did they give me? Parcel-heaving at the railway station (or, for younger readers, the train station). I limped in to report to P.H.G. (Postman, Higher Grade) Alf. At that time a popular television western series, I think it was the 'The High Chaparral', included a character with a wooden leg, whose name was Chester. "Oh look, it's Chester!" cried Alf on seeing me limping in to work for the first time and that remained my name for the rest of my G.P.O. employment. Alf decided that with my leg in plaster, I could not really be expected to heave sacks full of parcels on to a railway goods wagon and I was given light duties, such as writing tags indicating the addresses of the various local parcels offices around the country. There was one other student employee with me called David Harbour. David was an art student and so, of course, had the hairstyle required for that particular branch of study. David's long locks were a source of constant amusement for Postman Higher Grade Alf. "If you're going to the barber's," he would enquire, "do you ask for an estimate first?" or "When you go for a haircut, do you have gas?"

The other temporary postal workers were the men who usually dealt with the telegraph wires and poles, but were seconded to parcels during the Christmas rush. I think what they usually did was what the 'Wichita Lineman' in the Glenn Campbell song got up to, but I may be wrong. That is how I picture the Wichita Lineman at work anyway. These men regarded the parcels work as a holiday and their sole aim was to get the job done so quickly, that there would be time to go to the pub between loads. To do that, they had to break the rules. It was night-time and the officials were all in bed. The lorries bringing the parcels from the main post office were meant to park in the station forecourt, where its sacks would be unloaded into small wagons, which would then be manually wheeled into the goods yard for loading into the waiting railway goods trucks. That all took too long as far as the linemen were concerned. They would drive their trucks straight across the rails and directly up to the goods wagons, saving at least half an hour for each load. I do not imagine the lorries' tyres lasted very long. In the pub I would be told, "No, you don't have to buy a round, Chester. You're a stoodent!"

Sometimes late at night we would take the registered mail to Cheddington station in adjacent Buckinghamshire. Once there, we had to load the mail into a net, which would be 'caught' by the mobile post office train as it passed without stopping. One night the train was going too fast. It burst the net and sent registered mail fluttering all over the tracks. We had to try and pick up all those precious registered envelopes in the dark.

Where we did that was very close the spot where, almost exactly a year later in 1963, Ronnie Biggs and his gang would carry out 'the Great Train Robbery'.

During another vacation I worked as a farm hand on the Gorhambury estate, just outside St Albans, where we lived then. The farm was part of Lord Verulam's four thousand acres, all within twenty five miles of London's Marble Arch. The most unpleasant part of the job was mucking out the pigs. The stench was so intense, that, when I tried to breathe through a lighted cigarette, in order to reduce the smell, I was totally unaware of its smoke. The worst moment came when another farm hand heaved some afterbirth into the middle of the pig shit, shouting, "Put that in the spreader too."

The best bit of the farm job was driving a tractor while harrowing a field. I was standing at the side of that field, surveying my handiwork, when a purely eighteenth century scene took place. There I was, a ploughboy on the Earl's estate, when who should pass by, riding his horse, other than the Bishop of St. Albans , still wearing his purple cassock and clerical collar. If I'd had a forelock, I'd have tugged it on the spot.

But I was not always a lowly peasant on the estate. A couple of vacations later via the wonderfully-named scholastic agents, Gabittas and Thring, I was hired to be tutor to the eleven year old Viscount Grimston, son of Lord Verulam. Reluctantly, the butler had to let me in by the front door of Gorhambury. It was probably a good thing that he didn't know that the year before I had been a farm-hand on one of the family's farms. Little Lord Grimston was a very clever boy and certainly did not need any 'cramming' for an exam. I was really a sort of male nanny. My job was to keep him amused with such activities as bowling to him in the nets, which I did incredibly badly, driving him to watch cricket at Lord's cricket ground and taking him water skiing. On one occasion his mother, Lady Verulam, accompanied us to the lake in Rickmansworth, so that Johnny could water-ski.

Lady Verulam was elegant, witty and very much the lady. As little Lord Grimston was enjoying himself, skiing round and round the lake, Lady Verulam turned to me and said,"Roger, we must get back. Please call Johnny in."

I shouted and bellowed, but could not be heard above the sound of the motor boat's engine. "Let me try", said Lady V. and, putting elegantly manicured finger and thumb to her lips, produced possibly the most piercing wolf whistle I have ever heard. It had an instant effect. Johnny stopped skiing.

Their stately home was, strictly speaking, open to the public. That was to comply with some tax agreement, but no great effort was made to attract visitors. However, some keen tourists would occasionally make their way up the two-mile drive to the house. There were no guides, so butler, family or anyone else available would do the conducted tour. One day some visitors arrived to view the house and Lady V challenged me to conduct the tour. I had managed to acquire enough knowledge of the house's contents and history to sound plausible and to my relief none of the visitors asked any questions.

I was secretly rather taken by one of Johnny's elder sisters, the beautiful Lady Romayne Grimston. So, when she told me that more than anything in the world, she wanted a temporary bus-stop sign to put in her bedroom, I was a knight on an errand. Driving warily round the local Hertfordshire countryside, I managed to locate the object of her desire in a deserted leafy lane somewhere and, in a swift drive-by operation, managed to seize the bus stop sign. I hope the buses continued to stop there.

At the end of one of my 'tutor' stints, Lady Verulam presented me with a pot of honey, which had something wrapped round it. Examining the pot, I discovered that an elastic band held the cheque for my wages and a five pound note. I did not get the literary reference at first. Then 'The Owl and the Pussycat' came into my head. "They took some honey and plenty of money wrapped up in a five pound note".

What a delightful family!

More down-to-earth was driving a baker's van in St Albans. It required an early start and the smell of the freshly-baked bread was irresistible. Having had no breakfast, I would open the little door behind the driver's seat, seize a bit of loaf and stuff it into my mouth. That would inevitably be followed by a bout of hiccoughs, which would interrupt the flow of my sales pitch.

"Would you like any (hic) cakes this morning, Madam?"

I was advised by one of the other drivers to pay particular attention, if one of the housewives should ask me, "Have you got a long one, Baker?"

Before I started doing my rounds, the boss took me for a drive to show me which houses I should call at, where to park, where to drive forwards and where to reverse. There was an 'unadopted' avenue of rather posh houses close to the cathedral. I was told to turn round at the start of the avenue and to reverse up it to the last house. I did that regularly, until one day I noticed a lot of broken glass in the recommended turning spot. To save the van's tyres I drove forwards up the avenue, deciding I would reverse out. There were only wing driving mirrors and I managed to back the van into an unaligned and unseen tree. The boss sacked me. I was only trying to save his van's tyres.

When I was not tutoring, driving a baker's van or working in the Post Office, I would often go to stay at the Devon cottage of Trinity friend, Chris Hart, for a boating and drinking holiday. Chris had an enormous Great Dane dog called Thor. When we took the ferry across the water into Salcombe, Thor would usually accompany us and his size was a great talking point for our fellow passengers.

"Ooh, he's big, isn't he?" "Does he need a lot of exercise?", "How much does he eat?"

Another Chris, Chris Serle, who is very tall, would often come to stay as well. One day we were on the ferry without Thor, but with tall Chris. I started asking Chris Hart some pertinent questions about tall Chris.

"He's very big, isn't he? Does he need much exercise? How much does he eat?", etc.

Chris Serle joined in by doing nothing except staring out to sea, much as Thor would have done.

A Castle Called Gladys: I remember too, us building a magnificent sandcastle one day. We called the castle 'Gladis', which, for those who don't know, is pronounced 'Glaads' like Glamis. Gladis was attacked by a small boy on Salcombe Beach. He started smashing up our magnificent creation, but was soon chased away by Mike

Guilbride. The terrified boy fled, convinced that he was being pursued by the Totnes Monster.

Very silly!

On one of our lazy sea fishing outings, having caught several mackerel, we used some of those fish as bait in our search for something more ambitious. Having done nothing more skilful than to sit in the boat and watch my rod, I was rewarded with a sizeable fish, which Chris and Mike declared to the largest Red Gurnard they had ever seen. Thinking it might be a record local catch for the season, we took the unfortunate fish to have a possible record ratified at the Plymouth Marine Laboratory. The expert there examined our catch and declared to my disappointment that it was not a Red Gurnard but a specimen of the larger Grey Gurnard, that was unusually pink. I think I went unusually pink as well.

13.

ORTHOMORPHIC MYCORRHIZA

My father, while writing his books, also did some research for the Oxford English Dictionary. They were updating their massive 'complete' version, which consisted of twenty large volumes. As new words came into the language, the dictionary would employ various specialists. whose job was to try to find the earliest usage of the word in question. When he was too busy, my father would sometimes farm this job out to me. It was fascinating. 'Piedmont glacier' was one of the words I worked on. I got a pass for the library of the Royal Geographic Society in South Kensington. I had a bit of a triumph there, when I found a book containing the words, "I suggest the term 'Piedmont glacier' for this formation." That must surely have been the expression's earliest use.

There were also the words 'orthomorphic mycorrhiza', which I looked for in the Natural History museum library. I cannot remember if I had any success with that one but the words have stuck in my mind. The work took me sometimes to the famous Reading Room of the British Museum. The massive dome of the Reading Room causes a strange, repetitive echo. The sound of a cough or the placing of a book on a desk would reverberate round the room, creating what broadcasters call a 'flutter echo'. One evening when I was there, a power cut occurred and the entire library was plunged into darkness. I remembered a line from Gerard Hoffnung's 'Guide for London tourists' in which he asked, "Have you tried the echo in the British Museum Reading Room?" Here was my chance. Attempting to imitate the guide in the Duomo at Pisa, I sang the four notes of a chord, so that the result would be a harmonious echo. The power cut was reported in the next day's 'Guardian', which - rather unfairly, I thought, said "a desultory attempt was made at singing". I should have listened more carefully to that guide in Pisa.

Ardmore film studios were in Bray, not far from Dublin. Occasionally students were able to find work there as film extras for the princely sum of four pounds and ten shillings a day, at least double the daily allowance provided by a student grant. It was tedious work consisting of mostly hanging about, waiting for something to happen. The busiest person in the studio was someone referred to as 'P.J.'. Among P.J.'s duties was providing the effect of smoke via a special gun. Some of the scenes in the film of Somerset Maugham's novel, 'Of Human Bondage' were set in a smoky pub, where the director of photography would either complain that there was not enough smoke or that it was too smoky. The ensuing cry from an assistant director would be either, "Smoke it up, P.J." or "Kill the smoke, P.J."

An assistant director approached a group of us extras one day and asked, "Any of you lot actors?" I eagerly volunteered myself. The assistant director told me what I had to do, "When Miss Novak (Kim, the star) walks past your table, say to her, "Are you doing anything this evening, Mildred?". She will reply, "Have you asked your mother's permission?"" My line was kept in the final cut. My voice was part of a general hubbub, but I was able to distinguish my line and then Kim Novak's reply in a cockney accent worthy of Dick van Dyke.

14.

BBC RADIO

An important visitor came to see Trinity Players' summer revue in 1964. It was Peter Titheradge from the BBC, whose job title was 'Organiser Light Entertainment, Radio'. The BBC loves titles and, more than that, the initials that go with them. So, Peter was O.L.E.(R). Olé!

He spoke to me at length and suggested that I might like to apply for a six month 'training attachment' to his department at the BBC. He explained that Light Entertainment had searched the B.B.C. internally for candidates for the traineeships but had not felt satisfied with the applicants who came forward. Peter had visited various universities, interviewing potential recruits for the scheme. As far as I was concerned it was an offer I could not refuse and I carefully wrote an application without telling any absolute untruths. To my delight I was called for an interview. On the appointed day I set off for what had once been a popular concert hall in London's Bond Street, the Aeolian Hall, then headquarters of Radio Light Entertainment. I arrived at St Pancras station and asked a taxi-driver to take me to Aeolian Hall. Once I was in the cab, he slid his passenger window back and asked, "Where exactly is this 'Hole in the Wall', then, Guv?" I did reach the Hole in the Wall successfully and nervously waited for my interview with the Head of Light Entertainment, Roy Rich. Peter Titheradge told me later that his boss had said about me, "Ordish seemed a bit shy to start with, but I soon loosened him up with a few four-letter words". That was not how I remembered it at all, but with colleagues we pictured his version of events: "So, Ordish, you want to join the f---ing BBC, do you?" I eagerly wanted to and did so. I stayed at the BBC for the next thirty- three years.

I was already cast to act in a revue that was due to run until October in Dublin and was able to fulfil that commitment before what was to be the start of my new life. My employment began on November the first, 1964. After six weeks or so of 'trailing' other producers and studying how radio programmes were made, I was entrusted with the job of producing one of Light Entertainment Department's simplest programmes. 'Roundabout' was a daily magazine programme, which was transmitted live on the Light Programme at 6.15 p.m. It consisted of music and talks. Each weekday's programme had a different presenter (We did not say 'disc jockey' then). The music was a mixture of records, brief talks and live or specially-recorded items from one of the residential quartets or quintets, such as Humphrey Lytttleton's jazzmen. My job was to choose the records, supervise the music and speech recordings, create the running order and make sure the live programme finished exactly thirty seconds before seven p.m.

The presenter of 'my' programme was old Etonian Tim Brinton, who later became an ITN newsreader and the M.P. for Gravesend, which he won in the Thatcher landslide of 1979.

Sitting on my right at the control panel of one of Broadcasting House's subterranean studios was the studio manager. I do not suppose she had much sympathy for this jumped-up producer, who had never been a studio assistant or a studio manager himself. (for younger readers the word 'sympathy' has almost universally been replaced by 'empathy'. I have not been able to discover the difference). Anyway, back in the studio: shortly before we went on air the studio manager turned to me and asked, "Would you like me to chase the fades?" I had no idea what she was talking about, but wanted to sound confident. Since 'chasing the fades' seemed to be an acceptable option, I replied, "Yes, please."It sounded like something from Greek mythology, but I discovered later what it really meant. If a record ended with musical fade, it was an option for the studio manager to 'chase' that fade, making it disappear more quickly than it did on the recording.

There were six new trainee producers, all enrolled within a year or two of each other and all in our twenties. One recruit, who left fairly soon, was a man called John Cleese. He wanted to pursue a career in television. I wonder what happened to him. Ultmately the most successful perhaps was David Hatch (later Sir David), who became second in command of the whole BBC, helping, I think, to mitigate the bureautic excesses of Director General, John Birt. In early days David, his wife and their new baby lived in a tiny, noisy high-rise flat near Heathrow. I remember staying the night there once, probably having consumed a lot at a jolly supper. I shaved with his razor the next morning and will always remember how blunt it was. Times were hard for him in those days, it seemed.

Shaving is a strange ritual. It used to distinguish us shavers from the 'Barbarians'. The ritual is fast going out of fashion. Beards are more or less compulsory now for any man under forty. Sell your shares in Gillette! What a strange thing fashion is. The trendsetters seem to be saying,

"Why can't you be different, like the rest of us?"

I enjoy shaving, especially the bit where you put a hot flannel on your face at the end of the shave. I once had a beard shaved off at London's top hairdresser's, Trumper's of Jermyn Street, who make it a delightful experience. Before applying shaving soap every day, I still splosh my face with a hot, wet brush and think of Trumper's.

Our 'gang' at Aeolian made it feel more like university than a place of work. We were still young enough to indulge in silliness. We constructed what we called 'the tank' entirely out of material from our offices. The body of the vehicle was an empty box, which had held two hundred cigarettes (a Christmas present from a record company - how times have changed!) The wheels were four 45 rpm demo discs, also courtesy of the record companies. The axles were standard issue BBC pencils and BBC elastic bands held the wheels in place The end of a sound recording tape was sellotaped to the cigarette box and the tape recording machine was placed in a corridor. Pressing the machine's start button caused the Tank to trundle in a wobbly fashion along the corridor to the triumphant music coming from the tape, Sousa's 'Stars and Stripes for Ever'.

One of the 'Roundabout' bandleaders was the delightful Sandy Brown, who, as well as being a brilliant clarinettist, was chief acoustic architect at the BBC. He was a very funny man and with John Cassels, another of us young producers, we could laugh the night away. One of our flights of fancy was an imaginary society, which we called 'the Monotony Club of Great Britain' set up in opposition to the Variety Club of Great Britain and dedicated to the championing and cultivation of the most boring things and people we could find. The club's motto was 'Per Ardua ad Nauseam' and the award for the most boring event or person was 'the Lead Zeppelin', named after a comedian's aside at the end of a bad joke, "That went down like a lead Zeppelin". One winner of the award was a book Sandy found. It was called 'A Hundred Years of Portland Cement'.

As a designer of recording studios, Sandy was in contact with some of the rock stars of the day. He probably mentioned the Monotony Club and the Lead Zeppelin to his customers. I cannot help thinking that indirectly that may have led to the band name, 'Led Zeppelin'.

Most people stop looking, when production credits start to appear on the television screen, which means that they generally go un-noticed, however important they may seem to us who are named in them. However, the radio listener cannot help but hear the names read out after a radio programme. When my relatively unusual surname started to be heard as the producer credit of 'Roundabout' for example, it would occasionally be absorbed into the listener's consciousness. My father was delighted, when a work colleague asked him if he was related to the radio producer called Ordish. "Yes. He's my son," he was pleased to reply.

Back in the days when 'encountering an issue' meant meeting one of your offspring, I was was still living with my parents in St Albans, although I had started working for the BBC. When my parents went away for Christmas, 1964. Chris Hart invited me to stay with his family for the festivities in nearby Radlett. On Christmas Day, being unknown in their area, I was asked to be Father Christmas. I was given a splendid outfit to wear and sent to do the rounds of various houses nearby with children of appropriate ages. The parents would occasionally offer Father Christmas a small tipple. I usually declined, knowing that there would inevitably be a lot of drink on offer during the rest of the day. Christmas Day brings a wonderful suspension of disbelief and Father Christmas walking in the road gets cheery greetings from nearly every passer-by. My F.C. duties done, Chris and I drove to St Albans, where my father's ninety year old mother was staying for Christmas at a retirement home, while my parents were away. In the car we rehearsed harmonising a few well-known carols to sing to her. Granny was sharing her accommodation with a younger 'minder', a Mrs. Gregory. Chris and I shouted our harmonies to my fairly deaf grandmother, who seemed to enjoy our offering. My mother told me later that, when they went to collect grandmother from the retirement home, she had said to Mrs. Gregory, the companion, "I believe my son and his friend came and sang some carols for you on Christmas Day," "Yes," repled Mrs. Gregory, "Well, you have to put up with that kind of thing at Christmas, don't you?".

Going right back to the days of 'Sister George' ,the BBC always had a fair number of lesbians on the staff, more than their distribution in the population as a whole, would be my guess. One thing I noticed about many of them was that they were always having to tell the world of their gender preference. Whatever the topic of conversation, references to lesbianism would somehow find their way into the conversation. A friend and I invented this little exchange:

ME: "Morning, Mary. Nice day today!"
MARY: "Not for us lesbians, it isn't."

15.

RICHMOND, SURREY

The best Chinese restaurant in Richmond, Surrey, where fellow radio producer John Cassels and I shared a flat, was the Richmond Rendezvous. The head waiter there was the wonderfully inscrutable Henry Tsang. The general practice then was for Chinese people in the U.K. to take an assumed English first name - to make life easier for the natives, I suppose. The names they chose were usually slightly out-of-date names like 'Henry', 'Albert' or 'Earnest', although today those Victorian names are creeping back into fashion. I met a one year old boy the other day, who is called Sydney and even Sid for short. Back at the Chinese restaurant, a rather pompous friend summoned Henry over one evening, showed him the menu and enquired, "Henry, tell me, what exactly is the difference between 'Duck and Asparagus' at eighteen and sixpence and 'Duck and Asparagus, special Peking-style' at a guinea?'" Henry Tsang pondered for a moment and then replied inscrutably, "Same food, different price". I think today it is called 'marketing'.

Talking of Chinese restaurants, it puzzles me that the brilliant Chinese, who seemed to have invented just about everything from gunpowder through paper to tofu, never got round to inventing the fork.

Light Entertainment produced one programme a week for the BBC World Service. For a few months I was allocated to be in charge of it. 'Outlook' was, a weekly magazine programme, not unlike 'Roundabout' but a bit more serious. The World Service claims audiences of over a hundred million listeners. It was an amazing thought that one's transmissions were reaching such vast numbers. My boss at Bush House in the Strand was an old-style BBC stalwart, Bob Gregson, once described as 'the last of the

Reithians' (LordReith was the first director general of the BBC). I would occasionally be summoned to meetings in Bob Gregon's formidable presence. His title was 'Head of World Service', but he was referred to internally simply as 'Head of World'. Many years later there was a correspondence in the Times newspaper about grandiose job titles. I wrote this letter to the editor:

"Sir, When I was a BBC radio producer in the Sixties, I was occasionally summoned to meetings with the man who was in charge of the BBC World Service. He was always referred to internally as 'Head of World'. I decided that, if I should meet a Martian, who demanded,"Take me to your leader", I would know where to send him, "Oh, you want to pop along and have a word with old Bob Gregson in Bush House."

Not only did they publish my letter; it was chosen for an anthology called 'Times Letters of the Year, 1997'.

GRUMP - TATTOOS

Typically , as a Grumpy Old Man, I abhor tattoos. It baffles me why anyone should want to stain their bodies permanently in this hideous way. It is like buying a shirt (and usually a very ugly shirt), that you have got to wear every day - and night - for the rest of your life. It might have seemed a hilarious idea on that drunken Ibiza holiday to have a dotted line and 'slit here' tattooed round your neck, but thereafter you will have to wear a polo neck jumper at job interviews. Even discreet tattoos bearing erotic messages may lose their appeal, when the wearer is screaming on the bed in the delivery room, about to give birth to her fourth child.

16.

BBC TELEVISION

In 1967 the opportunity arose for BBC Radio employees to apply for what was called an 'attachment' to the equivalent of our department, but in television, an opportunity not to be missed. I applied and was accepted. I rented a bed-sitter in Royal Crescent, Holland Park, from where it was possible to walk to work at White City. We attachees were first required to take the television directors' training course, which was wonderfully informative. We received lectures from, amongst others, David Attenborough and Huw Wheldon and learned the basics of television production. At the end of the three weeks each of us had to prepare and direct a ten-minute production exercise. I presented a sketch show, whose cast included David Hatch, later to be Managing Director BBC Radio.

Another job I had during my attachment to television was to act as the production assistant on a 'pilot' programme with disc jockey, Alan Freeman. It was an attempt to do for television what the BBC had just started to do on the newly-created Radio One. It did not work, but our pilot programme was recorded in the BBC's Manchester studio, which was then a converted suburban church. This was long before the forced relocation of hundreds of BBC staff to the totally unnecessary £800 million pound establishment in Salford, Manchester. Our boss, Bill Cotton Junior, came up to Manchester to see the recording of the pilot and he joined the team for dinner after the show. It had been decided that the New Year's Eve programmes that winter would for the first time ever not be coming from Scotland and Bill was searching for a show title that was nothing to do with Hogmanay or heather. At that time there was a strangely named series of shows being transmitted by our department, featuring famous, established comedians. The shows were called for instance: 'Suddenly It's Arthur Askey' or 'Suddenly it's Max Bygraves'. Bill asked the assembled table, "What am I going to call our New Year's Eve variety show?" There was a silence, until I piped up with, "How about 'Suddenly It's 1968'?" Bill looked at me. "What did you say your name was?" he asked with a smile. That little moment may have been what got me a permanent job in television. The following week producer of 'Suddenly It's..' came up to me in the BBC club and was very annoyed about the pinching of his programmes' title. Suddenly it wasn't a happy Albert Stevenson.

Albert had been a prisoner of war in Japan. I think he was in the notorious Changi, where my cousin was, which must have been an unbelievable hell for him. A few years later a group of Japanese television executives was visiting the BBC and they were being entertained in what was called 'the Waitress Service Restaurant'. Unfortunately Albert was having lunch there at the same time. There was a Japanese flag on the visitors' table. Albert strode from his chair, marched up to the visitors' table, seized the Japanese flag and stamped on it repeatedly. The episode was hushed up, but, having heard of the horrors of Japanese prisoner camps, I could not help but see Albert's point of view.

After I had taken the directors' course, I still had five months 'attachment' to the entertainment department of BBC television. Some of that time was spent 'trailing' productions from rehearsal through to the studio day. I was also given the job of researcher on what we would now call a chat show (or is it gabfest?) It is a very interesting job, since it entails visiting famous or interesting people, who are about to appear on the show and providing the background of the interviewee and a suggested list of questions for the presenter, questions that you hoped would receive the most informative answers.

One of my research jobs was to interview Desmond Morris about his hugely popular new book, 'The Naked Ape', now slated as sexist and just about everything-elsist. I had to make notes about him and suggest suitable questions for the presenter, Simon Dee, to ask. On the day of the book's publication I telephoned to arrange a meeting. Desmond Morris suggested we meet in Hatchard's book shop in Piccadilly. "At the same time I can see how the book is selling." he told me. As any good researcher should, I had already read 'The Naked Ape' as a pre-publication edition from McGraw, its publishers. I took the book along with my notes to Hatchards, went into the shop and looked around for Dr Morris. No sign of him. I waited and waited. No mobile phones in those days, so I decided to find a phone box and call him. I made to leave the shop.

"Excuse me, sir," asked an assistant, "Have you paid for the book?"

"No," I replied, "I brought it in here with me."

"But it has only been published today."

"Yes. This is a pre-publication copy," I explained.

"If you already have the book," said the assistant, growing a little sterner, "May I ask why you have come in here?"

"I have an appointment to meet the author."

"But he doesn't appear to be in the shop, does he?" asked my interrogator, looking around.

"No," I replied feebly. It did sound a very unlikely story, I must say, but at that very moment, who should walk into Hatchard's but Dr Desmond Morris. When the author was between me and the assistant, I pointed at Desmond Morris and gave the assistant a wide, artificial grin. "See, I told you!" I mouthed.

Peter Noble was a freelance journalist, who - amongst many things - wrote a weekly article for an Indian English language film magazine about the latest goings-on in Tinseltown. From his flat in London's Maida Vale he would write such lines as, "Guess who I bumped into on Sunset and Vine last week? Only Robert Redford!"

Peter would come to our production meetings and could sometimes help us find star guests, whose latest movie was about to be released. He was late arriving at one of these meetings, because he had just returned from the Cannes Film Festival. Someone asked him, "How was Cannes, Peter?", to which he replied, "Marvellous darlings, and all the stars send their love."

I recently compared the sizes of production teams then and now and it seems as if the number of people involved in the making of a programme has increased at almost the same rate as the number of bosses in the BBC. The Graham Norton chat show probably is the nearest modern equivalent to the Simon Dee programmes of the late sixties. Here is a table of the production teams for comparison:-

	Graham Norton	Simon Dee
Researchers	3	3
'Production Team'	3	2
Scriptwriters	2	1
'Script coordinator	1	0
'Production co-ordinator'	1	0
'Line producer'	1	0
Producers	3	1
'Talent producers'	2	0
Commissioning Executive	1	?
'Head of Production'	1	0
Executive producer	1	0
'Series producer'	1	0
Director	1	1

For Graham Norton's show there were seven people with the title 'producer'. It is hard to imagine what they all do. Sit and squabble all day?

For the Simon Dee show there was only one producer and, while I had the job, I had to direct the programme as well. And it was live. The programme was, if anything, more complicated than Graham Norton's programme, since there could be as many as four live music slots as well as three or four interviews. A show that was memorable for us, was one, in which Sammy Davis Junior made an appearance. We could not be sure if he was going to turn up or not and had Peter Noble as a 'stand-by guest' on call. To get one of the 'Rat Pack' as a guest at the height of their fame would be a coup for us. I told a researcher to visit Sammy Davis and, if possible, stick with him all day and persuade him to do the show. As the studio clock was ticking down to zero, there was still no sign of Sammy or the researcher. I was in the director's chair.

After the start of the transmission and during the first interview the floor manager whispered to me up in the gallery that Sammy Davis had finally arrived. We were live on air. A minute or so later Max Harris, the musical director, came through on his talkback, to me, saying, "Sammy Davis has just arrived in the band area. He wants to sing a song, "This Guy's in Love with You" and has handed me the music parts. Unfortunately the arrangement is for strings and, as you know, we don't have any strings." I was trying to listen to Max at the same time as saying things like, "Coming to the wide shot on camera four".

In the end Sammy did sing his song, for which there had been no rehearsal, of course. Sammy went and stood any old where, while the lighting director tried to find the nearest lights to light him. The brass and woodwind players in the orchestra improvised from the string parts and the sound supervisor made it up as he went along. The finished product was amazingly good and was a tribute to the skill of British musicians and BBC technicians. I rang 'continuity', the people in charge of feeding programmes to the transmitters and asked if we could overrun by a couple of minutes, but they were Jobsworths and took us off the air, so that they could run an non-vital trailer for 'Doctor Who'.

For a while I directed Bruce Forsyth's 'Generation Game', which was quite 'hairy', since we did not know what the contestants or Bruce were going to do next. If I remember rightly, there were only four cameras, four contestants, Bruce and, ideally, a wide shot. The show was pre-recorded, but had to be shot 'as live', since re-takes were not really possible. The potter's wheel featured every now and then, since we knew the contestants would provide some suitably disastrous results and an opportunity for Bruce's repartee. There was one contetant, who looked at the sad pile of clay slumped on his wheel and said to Bruce, "It's a bit puckered, I'm afraid," Buce retorted, "I'd say it was well and truly puckered."

The games that the contetants had to play and compete in were always given a name, by which Bruce Forsyth would introduce them. 'The next game's called 'Icing a Cake', or what ever it was going to be. Our floor manager for the Generation Game was the lovely Chris Breeze. Chris was a bit older than most of us working on the programme and wore glasses and hearing aids. These appendages made life a bit complicated at the start of Chris's studio day. He would have to remove his glasses and his hearing aids in order to insert the earpiece that was his communication line to the director's gallery. Then he would attach his radio microphone, test the earpice and replace his glasses. The whole process involved a certain amount of juggling with wires and devices. Observing this one morning, Bruce announced, "And the first game's entitled, 'Assembling Chris Breeze'.

We would invent other imaginary games for the programme: "Right, behind you you will see the hindquarters of six well-known animals and in the trays in front of you are their droppings. All you have to do is put on your rubber gloves and place the right droppings in the right orifice. Music, please, Ronnie. You've got two minutes, starting from now."

Or. "The next game's called 'autopsy'. Here's your scalpels. Now, what did he die of?".

17.

CHELSEA

At that time I was in effect the lodger in the splendid Chelsea house of a BBC colleague, David Mallet, who went on be described later in life as 'arguably the most experienced live music director in the world'. If I remember rightly he was even then (1968) already directing 'Top of the Pops' for the BBC at the age of twenty-three. His enthusiasm for pop music television started when he was still at Winchester College. Jack Good, the very successful producer of such TV shows as 'Six-five Special' and 'Oh Boy!' went on to produce a hit series in the U.S.A., 'Shindig'. Jack Good gave a talk at Winchester and David was able to speak to him about their shared passion. Jack Good told David that, if he could pay his own air fare, he could come and do what would now be called 'work experience' with him in Hollywood. David was very much the baby son of Sir Victor Mallet, whose mother had been had been a maid of honour to Queen Victoria. Sir Victor was a godson to Queen Victoria. Perhaps he was named after her. The family seemed to span centuries. Sir Victor had had a very distinguished diplomatic career, being envoy to Sweden during World War ll, a critical posting, and ambassador to Spain and then to Italy after the war. He was fifty-two when David was born. David persuaded one of his much older brothers to ask his father if he could take up the work experience offer from Jack Good. Sir Victor considered for a moment and then enquired, "This man Good: is he a bugger?"

This man Good wasn't a bugger and David went to Hollywood. David's house was in Bywater Street, Chelsea, where also lived renowned producer, Ned Sherrin, of 'That Was the Week, That Was' fame. Ned was producing a series of sketch shows by playwright N.F. Simpson called 'World in Ferment' and I was directing it.

Ned's renown and influence were such that he was able to persuade several famous names to take cameo roles in the series. For me, more impressive than working with the latest pop stars, was to find myself in the rehearsal room, directing actors, whose names I knew from my childhood, Wilfred Pickles for instance. Also taking roles in 'World in Ferment' were Irene Handl, John Bird, Roy Kinnear and Dudley Moore. Irene Handl played a character called Madame Astoria, who was reverentially interviewed by Doug Searchbaker, played by Dinsdale Landen. Madame Astoria had been 'the world's most famous Woolworth's supervisor'. Had she ever met royaty, asked Dinsdale. "Oh, yes," replied Irene Handl, "King George the Fifth and Queen Mary visited the shop and I shall never forget their words. His Majesty came over to speak to me, but Queen Mary interrupted him saying. 'I think you've already spoken to that one.'"

We filmed the Madame Astoria interviews in David Mallet's house in Bywater Street, for which he received a fee. Convenient for David, me, and for Ned Sherrin.

The most delightful programme to produce was 'Call My Bluff'. To get to know the cast, I had separate working lunches in the BBC canteen with with presenter, Robert Robinson and the two team captains, Frank Muir and Arthur Marshal, who each informed me that the other two were 'slightly mad' but there never was any friction in the studio and we recorded only two thirty minute programmes in the studio day. Nowadays probably five episodes would be recorded in a day. The simple principle of the game was that each team gave three apparent dictionary definitions of obscure words from the twenty volume Oxford English Dictionary (the one I had contributed to), the opposing team having to identify which definition was the true one. The participants were able to see in advance the definitions they would be reading out. The actor, Richard Briers, was in an episode that comes to mind. He asked to have a word with me and I went to see him in his dressing room.

"Look. I'm sorry, but I dont think I shall be able to say this word without bursting into giggles. Can I have a different word?"

The word was PRUNT, which incidentally means a small blob of glass fused to another piece of glass.

WINE GROWING IN ENGLAND

George Ordish

NO. 3 IN THE COUNTRYMAN LIBRARY

Father's wine-growing book. Child labour on the wine-press.

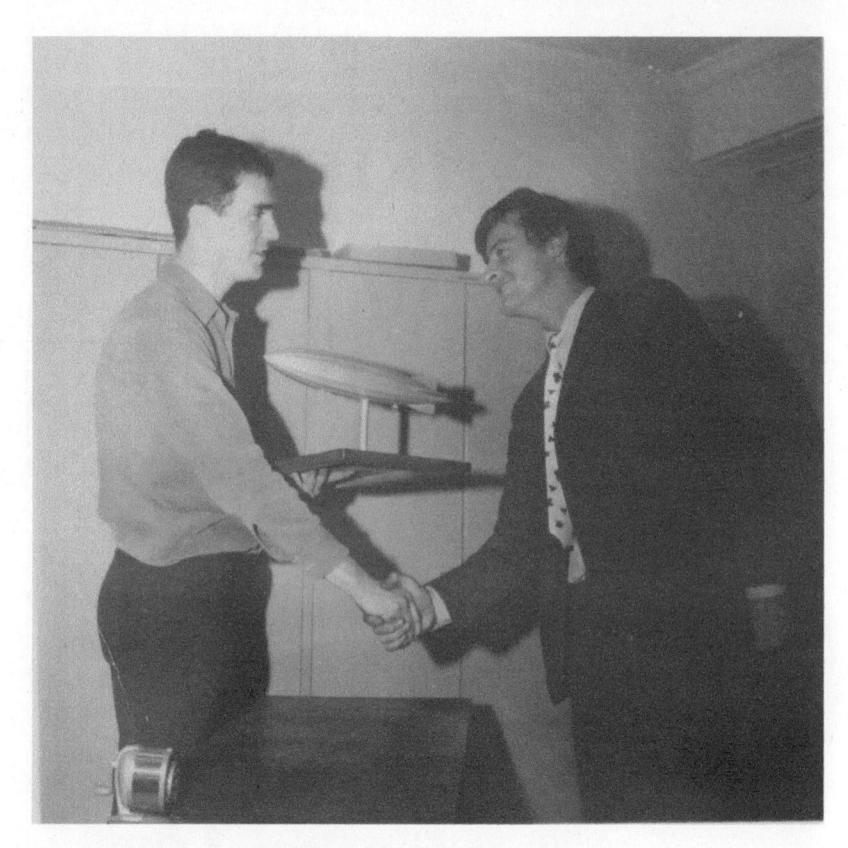

David does not realise that...

...the Zeppelin Award is made of lead.

The Albanian delegation.

The author with Pamela Hailstone beside her Greenland igloo.

Daughter Louise as 'Pinkie'.

Me with celebs and 'fixee'. Whatever happened to hindsight?

18.

SONG CONTEST

Before it became the partisan event it now is, the Eurovision Song Contest was usually won by the most attractive song, regardless of where it came from. Now Scandinavians vote for Scandinavians and the Balkans vote for the Balkans and so forth. The United Kingdom could not possibly win nowadays, not having sufficient 'followers', as they say in the social media. But in 1967 the United Kingdom was the winner. Sandie Shaw earned many *'douze points'* with her song, 'Puppet on a String'. That meant that the following year the U.K. would be the host nation. Tom Sloan, our overall boss, was the executive producer and the event was to take place in the Albert Hall. Tom, an immaculately presented man with a stiff upper lip and an excellent war record, was famously not very keen on foreigners. Perhaps not the ideal man for the job. We learned from Bill Cotton, his deputy, that Tom was tearing his hair out at rehearsals in the Albert Hall, due to endless special requests from singers, agents and bandleaders from all over Europe. Bill suggested to a group of us that we should devise some harmless practical joke to play on Tom. We suggested posing as the envoys of some rogue state, trying to enrol in the song contest. What a perfect opportunity for being silly.

At that time Albania was not unlike what North Korea is today, a totalitarian communist dictatorship of an undernourished people. The idea of Albania being in the song contest was more or less unthinkable but that is who we decided to be. Tom Sloan knew the three of us by sight, which made disguise the first essential. In those days before the misery of outsourcing, the Television Centre was a microcosm of all the needs of the B.B.C. We were skilfully disguised with facial hair by the make-up artists and the Wardrobe Department provided us with the sort of clothes we thought Albanian songwriters and agents would wear. Bill Cotton telephoned Tom Sloan to tell him, "These Albanians turned up at your office, asking why they have not been called for rehearsal, so I sent them over to you at the Albert Hall. They're on their way".

I had noticed that, when one speaks through an interpreter, both parties tend to look at the interpreter, rather than at the speaker. The presence of an interpreter would prevent us from being examined too closely. As the spokesperson for the group, I was going to have to speak fake Albanian. I approached a university friend, Sue Arnold, who had just secured her first reporting job with 'the Daily Sketch'. Would she 'interpret' for us? Her reply was that she would love to do it and that it would give her a scoop for her paper. Her reservation was that she did not feel that she could manage the fake Albanian. I told her what I would be 'saying' and it was agreed that she would whisper her 'interpretations' of Tom's replies back to me. Having somehow commandeered a chauffeur-driven Rolls Royce, the ever inventive Tony James pushed us into the car, instructing the driver, "Albert Hall - front entrance!"

We learned later that Tom Sloan, observing our Rolls arriving, commented, "Well, at least they've got some money".

We were ushered into Tom's office. How long would the hoax last? We were introduced with our Albanian names and we bowed in order to hide our moustachioed faces as much as possible. Tom bowed back. I had learned a little Russian as an auxiliary subject at university and hoped that similar noises might pass muster as Albanian in the forthcoming gobbledegook.

"Na zhonia v'Albania shkoozi Albert Hall ayev song contyesti"
Sue Arnold addressed Tome Sloan, Tom looked at Sue.

"Mr Adrelini," she said, "wants to know why the Albanian delegation has not been called for rehearsal at the Albert Hall?"

SONG CONTEST

My friend and colleague, Jim Moir, who knew about the hoax, was working on the Song Contest. Out of the corner of my eye I could see his back. His whole body was shaking with suppressed giggles.

"Tell them" Tom thundered, "Tell them that Albania is not a member of the European Broadcasting Union."

Sue leaned over and whispered nothings to me. I replied.

"Mazh djollie enzo kavimappipe, zgonia, zgonia!"

"Mr Adrelini says," continued Sue calmly, "that, if you heard their song, you would find it so beautiful, that you would include it in the Song Contest."

"That is not the point," cried the exasperated Tom, "I can only repeat that Albania is not a member of the European Broadcasting Union!"

That was our cue to sing. Britain's entry that year was Cliff Richard singing, "Congratulations". That was the melody we sang, but with Albanian words, of course.

"Kongratulazzi, Kongrattulazzi!"

At that point Tom's P.A., Queenie, recognised one of the Albanians, Terry Henebery, rushed forward and tore off his false beard. Brian Whitehouse and I removed our facial hair and astrakhan hats. Tom did a marvellous double take. Instead of being in the slightest bit angry, he was delighted. "That my producers should go to all this trouble!", he crowed. We all piled back to the Television Centre, where in the club (of course) the whole thing had to be re-enacted for Billy Cotton Senior, who was there with his son.

There was a technical rehearsal that evening to make sure all the national juries could communicate with London. The story of our hoax had got round Europe and when the voting was practised for the following day's live transmission, the technicians standing in for the juries decided that it was Albania who won.

"L'Albanie, douze points!"

19.

PUBS ETC.

I had thirty or so happy years of social drinking, before I got into the bad habit of drinking too much. I loved the pub and the camaraderie of being in effect a 'member' of a cheerful club with friends from all walks of life. In the pub we were all classless - that is we were, after the 'saloon' and 'public' bars were abolished. I suppose, roughly speaking, the public bar was working class and the saloon bar, middle class. 'Ladies' if they went to a pub at all, would go to the saloon bar. When there were two bars, I generally chose the public bar. That is where I found jollier company and - anyway - that is also where the dart board was usually found. In the Sun Inn, Richmond, Surrey in 1965 the interior walls were knocked down and Saloon and Public became one bar, but old habits died hard. I remember once straying over to what had been the more refined saloon bar side of the pub. Buster Deacon, a Public Bar regular, yelled at me from a group of darts players,

"Oi! Get back on your own side!"

There were two regulars called Brian. One Brian was a painter and decorator. The other Brian never spoke about what he did, but we thought that he was a civil servant and we knew that he spoke fluent Russian. One day a regular came into the pub and enquired of the landlord, "Has Brian been in?"

The landlord replied, "Which Brian do you mean? Brian, the decorator or Brian, the spy?"

The BBC Club bar was for many people the nerve centre of Television Centre. Meetings and script conferences were often held there. Eric was one of the commissionaires, who sat at the entrance and came in to the club to page drinkers, whose offices knew exactly where a missing person could be found. Eric would announce sonorously the name of the person sought. It is said that he once requested over the Tannoy that the cast of 'the Woodentops' should return to the studio.(I should perhaps inform younger readers that 'the Woodentops' was a programme featuring only animated puppets).

On another occasion Eric walked into the smaller of the two bars, where I was, and called for 'Mr Roger Reece'. I did not know of a Roger Reece, but knew a Roger Race and said to Eric, "Do you perhaps mean Roger Race, Eric?"

Eric looked at me and said nothing. A minute or so later he returned to where I was, accompanied by a man, whom I did not know. Eric said to me, "This, sir, is Mr. Roger Reece."

Going back to saloon bars and public bars, when we lived in Yalding, the pub nearest to us was 'The Two Brewers' and of course in those days the pub had the two usual gradations of bar, 'public' and 'saloon'. But Yalding was more or less the centre of Kent's hop growing area and in September came hop-picking time. During hop-picking the denizens of the public and saloon bars had to mingle under one roof, because what had been the public bar became the Hop-Pickers' Bar. Hundreds of East Enders would descend on the village for two weeks of hard-working 'holiday', living in pretty basic corrugated iron sheds on the outskirts of the village. When the day's work was done, the thirsty pickers could not be blamed for passing the time in 'The Two Brewers' It was surely preferable to going straight back to those cramped, corrugated iron huts. The village was in awe of these 'rough' visitors and the shops would install a chicken wire barrier on top of their counters, trying to deter any temptation to shop-lift. I hope the hoppers did not realise that this netting was there only when they were. At chucking-out time from the pubs we children would be awoken by a horde of happy hoppers singing such old favourites as 'We Ain't got a Barrel of Money' as they wended their wobbly way back down the road towards the sheds.

20.

BACKWARDS

I think it was on her third birthday that my younger sister. whom we call 'Ba', received a very special birthday card from the U.S.A. We were still in the middle of just-post-war austerity and rationing. I do not know if British birthday cards were even coloured then but Ba's birthday card was not only coloured - it was a musical box that played, 'Happy Birthday to You'. We had never seen (or heard) anything like it. Today such a musical card would contain a little file that would play the tune electronically, but this card was a real musical box containing the equivalent of a little xylophone, which would strike the required notes as you turned the handle. In America maybe a well-heeled child would throw such a toy away on the day after her birthday, but Ba's musical box took pride of place in our toy cupboard. We did not just play it on birthdays; we played it every day. It drove our parents mad. When I say we knew the tune backwards, I mean that literally, because with a real musical box, if you wind it clockwise, it plays the tune, but, if you wind it anti-clockwise, it plays the tune backwards. We could all sing the tune backwards.

The scene dissolves to a B.B.C. Radio office in Bond Street, London, some fifteen years later, where a young radio producer (me) is editing on a tape recorder some 'vox pop' interviews he has just conducted outside in Bond Street. He notices that, when he runs the tape backwards, some of the sounds are identifiable. For example the sound of 'you' played backwards approximately equals the sound of 'we'. Now, here was a chance for some silliness.

Breaking it down, the two vowel sounds in 'you' are 'ee' and 'oo'. Forwards they create 'eeoo' (you); backwards they create 'ooee' ('we'). Remembering my little sister's musical box birthday card, I hummed the memorised backwards tune of 'Happy Birthday' into the microphone and then reversed the tape. Out came the familiar birthday melody. Now to master the words.

Vowels are OK. Consonants present a problem. If you play backwards a recording of the word 'cat', it does not emerge as 'tac', because, however cleanly you say it, there is a small explosion or 'plosive' after the T. The word 'cat' in reality is closer to 'cats'. The reverse is therefore something like 'stack'. It is very complicated but fascinating to me, if not to most. The best way to cover the impossibility of speaking backwards perfectly is to make the performance be a known song (of which you have to learn the tune backwards, of course). The familiar melody covers the shortcomings of your reverse speech. At this point you may be muttering to yourself, "What on earth is he talking about?". To bring the matter to a close, here is what I call a sonic palindrome:

"We won, Bob, now you."

You might like to try this: Record the words, "We won, Bob, now you", play the recording backwards and the sound which comes out will be recognisably, "We won, Bob, now you." What a wonderful waste of time! But was it?

I did a couple of paid appearances on national television, performing my party trick, singing firstly, 'Happy Birthday' backwards, which begins, "oo yoot yedthirb ippah...". For my second appearance, I extended my repertoire to include (part of) 'I'm dreaming of a White Christmas'. That begins, "Tiaw eeb sisamzirk o:ee.." David Jacobs, host of his own chat show, approached me after my performance, asking (by arrangement), "Is that the end?", allowing me to reply, "No. That was the beginning."

My very good friend, David Mindel, asked me to perform the party trick at his wife's twenty-first birthday celebration and the weird performance must have stayed in his mind, because, many years later, when David had written one of his many television commercial jingles, this time for a beer ad, he got in touch. He knew that the plot of the advertisement involved filming people talking backwards. He told the producer of the commercial that he knew an expert in the art of back-talk.

I was hired. Contrary to what people may think the B.B.C. is fairly frugal in its expenditure on the actual making of programmes. Where the money is wasted is paying the army of bosses, heads of this and that and assistant heads of the other. When away filming, a B.B.C. crew will usually stay in the most economical hotels and generally eat and drink frugally. Filming a television commercial, we were put up in a five star hotel. It came as a shock to me, when I saw how the crew making a TV commercial operated. For a start, they filmed on thirty-five millimetre film, such as is used on Hollywood epics. On a 625 line television screen I defy anyone to see the difference between 35mm film and the much more economical 16mm film that we used in those days. The script for the commercial described the setting as 'a typical English beach', so where did we go? Marbella, of course. It was costly to make a bit of the Costa del Sol's sand look like Margate, but it was worth the trip, because of the weather, they said. Ah, yes, of course. The weather. It actually rained so badly in Marbella, that, on the first trip, filming was cancelled altogether and we had to go back home and get paid all over again two weeks later. Taking some days off as part of my 'annual leave', I somehow managed to fit it all in with my regular BBC duties.

The script involved the actors walking backwards across the beach while they spoke. In the background various events were taking place, such as a speedboat travelling across the sea. In the final version the people would appear to be walking forwards and talking forwards, while the speedboat towing a water-skier would appear to be travelling backwards. My job was to try to get the actors to say their lines backwards as accurately as possible, so that their lip and tongue movements would synchronise with what they were saying, when the forward speech was dubbed on to the final version. I know. It's complicated, but it worked. However, I don't put, 'talking backwards' on my CV.

Arthur Mullard, known for roles in film and television as a thicko bruiser made an appearance on the live Simon Dee show. This is how the scriptwriter worded the sign-off for the ending of the programme:

SIMON DEE: Well, that's all we have time for but- just before we go - here is a word - for our French viewers.
[cut to close-up Arthur Mullard]
ARTHUR MULLARD: Fromage (which he pronounced 'frommidge')

There was a huge laugh from the studio audience. So much laughter, that Arthur was a little concerned. After the show he asked to speak to the producer (me).

"What's this 'frommidge', then?" he enquired, "is it summink dirty?"

I assured him it was not dirty, so it was a happy ending.

If I remember rightly, my university friend, Chris Serle and I did a comedy turn at a BBC party, where Esther Ranzten was present. As part of our routine we simulated the sounds of audio-tape editing, Chris was the editor and I was the sound of the tape, running fast and slowly, forwards and backwards. The editor had to remove an unnecessary cough. The performance must have gone well, because as a result of it Chris auditioned for and became one of the presenters of 'That's Life'. Right place and right time, leading to a successful small screen career for my dear friend, Chris. The party was in Gill Stribling-Wright's flat. Gill started her career as a secretary in our department. In her first interview with Bill Cotton he asked her what job she saw herself having in her future career at the BBC. Gill replied, "Yours". She more or less achieved that a few years later, when she was in charge of entertainment programmes at Southern Television.

In my early days at the BBC Television Centre I acquired the most extraordinary part-time job. Princess Lalla Aicha, sister of the King of Morocco, had been a pupil at the Folkestone language school, owned by the mother of David O'Clee, my Trinity friend and fellow BBC producer. The princess's brother, the new king, wanted her out of Morocco and had appointed her against her will to be the Moroccan ambassador to London. The embassy had decreed that the Princess was in need of some more English lessons. David was unable to take on the task and he asked me if I would like to teach the princess. The bizarre nature of the job made it an opportunity not to be missed. On Thursday evenings a chauffeur-driven Rolls-Royce would arrive at the Television Centre, driven by a sinister-looking man in a leather jacket. I felt sure he had a revolver in his pocket. He would drive me to the ambassadorial residence in Bishop's Avenue, where I would be ushered into the presence of Her Highness and her lady-in-waiting. In what I have read since about the princess, it seems that she was too enthusiastic about women's rights for her brother's autocratic tastes and he wanted Lalla Aicha to be anywhere but Rabat. She was therefore a reluctant ambassador and a reluctant student of English. While I was trying to steer the language round to English, the princess and her companion would speak only French, except on one occasion, when the companion made to leave the room and was issued a sharp command in Arabic. I guessed she was being told:

"Don't leave me alone with a man!".

She may have been a women's libber, but there were limits. Sometimes I would arrive at the Bishop's Avenue house to be told, "No lesson tonight. We shall be going instead to the Playboy Club in Park Lane". Gambling and drinking alcohol! What would her brother have said?

On the subject of princesses, a few years later I was directing another experimental chat show with the lovely Nanette Newman and the brilliantly inventive Graeme Garden. Nanette was good friends with Princess Margaret and had invited her to come to one of the recordings in what we called the Television Theatre, which had once been the Shepherds Bush Empire. Although this was an informal visit, I thought I ought to call my boss, Bill Cotton, to inform him of the royal presence. Remembering the Albanian hoax, he asked, "Is this a wind-up?" Could I be trusted? It was not a wind-up and the Princess Margaret arrived, accompanied only by Nanette Newman, without police escort, equerry or lady-in-waiting. In the dressing room Nanette asked her if she would like a drink. "Yes, please," replied the princess, "a whisky." Nannette looked at me. In our 'hospitality' we had only beer crisps and white wine, but I smiled and said, "Leave it to me." Next to the theatre was a fairly rough pub, 'The Shepherds Bush Hotel', which we irreverently called 'The Irish Embassy'. It would not have surprised me to learn that there were I.R.A. sympathisers in the bar but it was my only hope of procuring whisky for the princess. I dashed across the stage, through the scene dock and into a side-door of the pub. I recognised John, the barman, who used to work at the BBC Club and offer customers cut price meat that must have fallen off a butcher's van.

Could I have a double whisky and could I take the glass away with me, please? I thought it better not to say who it was for. Walking more steadily back through the theatre without spilling a drop, I arrived at Nanette's dressing room and handed the whisky to Princess Margaret. "Could I have some soda, please?" she asked. We did not have soda. Should I go back to the Irish Embassy? I decided not to."I'm afraid we don't have any, Ma'am," I said. "That's OK," she replied and, putting the glass of whisky under the cold tap in Nannette's dressing room basin, diluted to taste.

Nanette Newman was married to film director, Brian Forbes. I went to a drinks party at their house in Virginia Water, which was a star-studded event. Roger Moore was there and told a group of us a story about a minor car accident he had had in Switzerland. Neither Roger Moore nor the driver of the other car was injured but, as both drivers left their vehicles to exchange words, the Swiss driver of the other car recognised Roger Moore and said, "Ach nein! Null, Null, Sieben!" (Oh no! Double-0-seven!)

21.

PROGRAMMES

In 1969-70 together with Trinity colleague David O'Clee, who had joined the BBC in the same way as I did, co-produced a series of a 'new faces' sketch shows entitled, 'Don't Ask us – We're new here'. The cast included Richard Stilgoe and Maureen Lipman, who both went on to enormous success. Keeping an eye on us new producers was executive producer, John Ammonds, renowned for bringing Morecambe and Wise to the BBC. To some extent aping 'Rowan and Martin's Laugh-In' 'Don't Ask Us' included 'quickies', in which one of the cast would sing a line of a well-known song followed by a 'tag-line'. For example, Adrienne Posta standing behind a giant cloverleaf, sang, "I'm looking over a four-leaf clover,". The music cut abruptly and Adrienne, who was fairly short in stature, added, "That's why they call me short-arse,". Our executive producer intervened. "I don't think we should use the words 'short-arse'", he said. "'Short-house' would be more acceptable". In the transmission the euphemism was employed.

That summer another member of the cast, Frank Abbott, was on holiday in Cornwall, staying in the beautiful seaside village of Mousehole. He sent a postcard from there to John Ammonds, our executive producer. Frank had altered one letter on the multi-view card, so that it read, 'Greetings from Househole'.

Unforgettable was working with the Kenneth Williams. He is now best remembered for his roles in the 'Carry on' films, which is a shame, since those rather tacky vehicles did not give him much opportunity to show his considerable talent. In the late 1960s Kenneth had great success as the host of 'International Cabaret', which, as the title suggests, was a variety show of acts from overseas but what viewers seemed to like best were the little gems delivered by Kenneth between the acts. Quite logically Bill Cotton thought, why were we wasting huge fees and travelling expenses for foreign acts, when what people really liked about 'International Cabaret' was Kenneth Williams' pieces to camera. Bill decided that we should devise a show without the foreign acts and with more Kenneth Williams. The plan was that the programmes should be scripted by the brilliant Scottish comedy writer, John Law. He had been one of the contributors to the highly successful London stage revue, 'Pieces of Eight', other writers of that revue being Sandy Wilson, Peter Cook and Harold Pinter. My favourite John Law line, delivered ad lib in the BBC Club, was that he had been to an 'unusual pets' party, where his tin of salmon had won first prize. By the time 'The Kenneth Williams Show' was ready to start rehearsal, John Law was very ill and, having contributed an outline script, was unable to continue the job. A replacement writer came to our rescue, but was perhaps unable to recreate that rapport, which John Law had with Kenneth's unique style. Here is the entry in Kenneth Williams' published diary for the sixth of January, 1970:

'Roger Ordish in the viewing room played us the number two show. Very pleased with it I must say. Went up to have the congratulatory drink, when (scriptwriters) David Climie and Austin Steele came over and the former said, "You heard about John Law? He's dead" I was really shocked. So at last after five months in a coma, John is dead. He was actually only forty years old. I have no time for grief – only time to work on his writing of this series and make it funny, as he would have wanted it.'

The shows were not a success, perhaps they missed scriptwriter John Law's subtle touch, or maybe it was because Kenneth was on all the time and not just as the link man. Bill Cotton said perhaps it was because the programmes were 'all meat and no gravy'. It was not a disaster, but did not get the hoped-for audience size. That said, rehearsals were a treat. In his flat Kenneth Williams usually lived a strangely ascetic existence and would read a book there standing up at a lectern. He would not have a sofa in his flat, since he could not bear the idea that, sitting next to someone, his and their bodies might accidentally touch. But, when from this solo monastic life he burst into the rehearsal room in the morning, his other self would emerge and he would tend to talk non-stop for several minutes, regaling us with delightful anecdotes. At one point he was in the middle of reading Gibbon's 'Decline and Fall of the Roman Empire'. Nero, he told us, would play the lute endlessly to his courtiers, who had to feign enjoyment of his performances. The Greeks in Nero's entourage were more sophisticated than the fawning Roman courtiers, Kenny told us. I can still hear Kenneth's marvellous delivery when he said, "While the Romans cried, "Wonderful, Emperor, beautifully played!", a more cynical Greek courtier might say, "Yes, very nice, Nero," then, putting his hand in front of his mouth, Kenneth added as an aside, "Stupid c**t!"

We suggested a series, 'Kenny Popularises the Classics'.

One of Kenneth's unforgettable stories was about the trial of a notorious Victorian villain, Archibald Plum, who had been accused of murder. His trial was hot news in the papers and it was a great surprise when, due to insufficient evidence, the verdict was commuted to manslaughter. Kenneth then painted a picture of a middle class Victorian household, in which the maid heard the paperboy shouting the headline about Plum's reprieve. She wanted to tell the master of the house the news as soon as possible. It happened that the master was having a bath at the time. The maid looked through the keyhole of the bathroom and was presented with the sight of her naked employer standing up in the bath, legs apart, with his back towards the door. The maid shouted through the keyhole the words that her master took to be, "They're not hanging plumb!". The maid was sacked.

The person most unspoiled by fame and success that I ever worked with was surely Sir Terence Wogan. Genuine through and through, witty, kind and considerate. I was producer of some of his talk shows in the early eighties. A gem of a story connected with one of his programmes concerned Christine, the receptionist at the BBC Television Centre. One of Christine's jobs was to make loudspeaker announcements, when a taxi arrived at reception to collect a guest. A driver would approach Christine and murmur to her the name of the person he had come to collect. Christine would press her microphone key and drone in her rather piercing nasal tone 'Taxi for Mr. Smith, taxi for Mr Jones', and so forth. Possibly the most celebrated name to appear on Terry Wogan shows was none other than the Dalai Lama. His driver came to collect him after the recording and whispered to Christine that that he was there for the Dalai Lama. Christine switched on her microphone and announced loudly and nasally to the reception area, "Taxi for Mr. Lama!"

22.

MORE CHAT

Agents, or maybe their clients, sometimes got a bit greedy with the BBC and would start asking for pay rises. The ensuing bargaining would occasionally result in something like this: "We cannot increase her basic fee per show, but instead of booking her for thirteen shows at £2,000, we could book her for twenty shows at £2,000 and we'll find a slot for another seven shows." It would sound a good idea at the time, but no-one had thought about what those other seven shows would be. Derek Nimmo had one of those contracts. He was booked to do thirteen shows of a sitcom about monks called 'Oh, Brother' (or 'Oh, Bother' as I once saw it misprinted). Nimmo was contracted for seven more programmes without content. Rather than write off his 'dangling' fees, it was decided to try him out as the host of a chat show, 'If it's Saturday, it must be Nimmo', which had its moments. I was the director. The series involved a trip to the USA, where we filmed an episode with chat-show host, Dick Cavett in New York, which gave me the opportunity to stay briefly with my sister, Ba, who lived with her lawyer husband in the leafy suburb of Rye in Westchester County. They held a little party for me, at which friends gave me two memorable bits of advice. When they learned that we were going on to film in Las Vegas, one guest advised me, "Roger, when you are in Vegas, don't blow your wad," Another whispered piece of advice was, "Remember, Roger, you won't get laid in Las Vegas, unless you pay for it."

As things turned out, I didn't blow my wad in Vegas, but I did get laid without paying for it. That sounds cruder than it really was. The aptly named Rosemary Long was one of the famous Bluebell Girls, appearing then at Caesar's Palace. I went to interview this English rose to arrange filming the Bluebells the next day. It was all very romantic and could have led to something more permanent, if she had not been in Las Vegas, while I was in London. At six foot, Rosemary was only an inch shorter than me and had legs that went on forever. Early on in our conversation Rosemary asked me what my star sign was. I had noticed that, when a woman asked me that, it usually meant they were interested. In the end it was a might-have-been, but wonderful while it lasted.

Another Las Vegas memory that has filtered through to the present day was walking with Derek Nimmo through the casino in Caesar's Palace. The casino boasted 'the world's biggest slot machine', called in keeping with the Palace's Roman theme, 'Colossus Jackpotus'. Walking towards us across the casino was Tom Jones, then at the height of his fame and earning a fortune singing in Las Vegas. "Ah, h-hello Tom," stammered Derek. Tom Jones replied in his lovely Welsh accent, " 'Allo, Derek, you all right?"

Derek had never actually met Tom Jones before and he murmured to me after Tom had passed, "I had no idea that T-Tom Jones was a dwarf."

Before his American trip Derek Nimmo had appeared nightly in 'Charlie Girl', an immensely successful musical that ran for five years on the London stage. We would sometimes have our production meetings in Derek's dressing room in the Adelphi Theatre. A tannoy let him know what point the show had reached. Occasionally Derek would suddenly dart out of the dressing room, almost mid-sentence and seconds later we would hear his voice on the tannoy coming from the stage as he delivered his next lines. Equally suddenly, he would re-appear in the dressing-room, saying, "Where were we?" I am sure he did it to impress, but impress he did.

In the early days of Michael Parkinson's chat show, the programme named simply by his surname, we used to make filmed inserts on various random topics. In the 1970s about the time of the U.K.'s referendums on joining the Common Market, we took a film crew to a lorry drivers' 'Routier' café on a motorway in Northern France. The object was to find the reactions of the French to a typical British menu. I remember much laughter as we compiled and translated into French the *carte du jour* for the lorry drivers. On offer were, for instance, *Crapaud dans le trou* (toad in the hole), *la sauce favorie de Papa*, (Daddie's Favourite Sauce) and *Bulle et pousser de petits cris aigus* (bubble and squeak).

Later, as producer of the 'Parkinson' shows, I met a host of famous people, but the meetings were usually fairly short and would not provide the more extensive knowledge of someone that can be gained as a researcher. Yes, I shook hands with Muhammad Ali, Orson Welles and Fred Astaire. Yes, I managed to obtain a guitar for John Lennon, which he requested minutes before we started recording the show, but these were generally fleeting exchanges, that would not permit me later to answer the question, "what was he/she like?". There were exceptions. That wonderful actress, Edith Evans, renowned for her spectacular line from 'The Importance of Being Earnest,' "A handbag?", was a guest on the show and during her interview with Michael Parkinson, she said, "I am a very good cook, you know." Michael replied, "I bet you can't make a Yorkshire pudding."

"I can and I shall prove it," retorted Dame Edith.

Some weeks later an invitation arrived for Michael and Mary Parkinson to visit Edith Evans's house in Kent for a Sunday lunch, at which Yorkshire pudding, made by the Mistress of the house would be served. Luckily for me, Mary Parkinson was unable to attend and I went in her place. While glasses of sherry were being drunk in the drawing room, Edith Evans announced in stentorian tones that she was off to the kitchen to put the Yorkshire pudding mixture in the oven. A few minutes later she re-entered the room in a beautifully theatrical manner and announced to us in that highly imitable voice:

"There has been a disaster! I forgot to put any flour in the Yorkshire pudding!" She let that sink in and then went on to announce, "Instead we shall be having roast beef and savoury custard!" And so we did. Roast beef, roast potatoes, Brussels sprouts and savoury custard. But Michael Parkinson was right, when he bet her she could not make a Yorkshire pudding.

Another 'celeb', whom I did meet more extensively, was the Italian film star, Gina Lollobrigida. She was on the point of publishing a book of her photographs, 'Italia Mia'. She was not going to be in London long enough to be researched there and she wanted prints of her original photographs to be taken by hand from Rome to London. Reluctantly I volunteered that I should take on this arduous task and presented myself at La Lollo's Rome apartment one afternoon. She was very welcoming, offered me a drink

and we sat on a sofa for a long time, going through her pictures, while I prepared notes for Michael Parkinson's questions. Her photographs were beautiful but, when you have an expensive camera and all Italy to choose from, it is easy not to go wrong. Afternoon became evening and there did not seem to be anyone else in the apartment. I started to wonder. She was so friendly. Could I ask her out for a meal? Don't be ridiculous, Roger. She's the most famous film star in Italy, a screen goddess, a sex symbol My dreams for the evening came to an abrupt halt, when I heard the front door open, a very handsome Italian man came into the room and hugged Ms Lollobrigida. As they used to say in 'the News of the World', I made my excuses and left.

Due to the 'Parkinson' programme, I once shook the hand of one of my heroes, Duke Ellington, whose choice of name must be connected to the Duke of Wellington. I like to imagine a party, where some of the more curiously named jazz stars are gathered and it's my job to do the introductions. "Dizzy, I should like you to meet Muddy." "Hi, Fats, this is Slim". "Duke, have you met Earl?" "I see Smokey and Dusty over there with Cannonball. Let's join them."

23.

SAVILE

I first met Jimmy Savile, when I briefly directed 'Top of the Pops'. I was introduced to him and he said, "Put a paper bag over is 'ead; e's better lookin' than me!", a remark, which I was to hear at least a hundred times more addressed to various young men over the years Savile and I were destined to be working together. A few years later I visited Savile in his Scarborough flat, which was a sort of shrine to his late mother, 'the Duchess'. I wish he had not told me that the bed I was to sleep in that night had been her bed and that the adjacent wardrobe was full of her clothes, which he had dry cleaned every few months. I have since learned that several years later Louis Theroux was put up in the same bed and that the Duchess's clothes were still there and continued to have their trip to the cleaners. Does this merit a T-shirt for Louis and me?:

"I have slept in the Duchess's bed."

My boss, Bill Cotton, believed too much in Jimmy Savile. When Bill described his concept for the 'Fix It' programme to me, my reaction was that it was a brilliant idea but that Savile was the wrong person to front it. That was not because of any of knowledge of Savile's paedophilia, but because I felt he was inept at interviewing and had no rapport with his subjects, especially if they were children. He was too self-centred. That may be characteristic of a psychopath. I asked Bill to consider someone else as presenter. I went and had tea with that brilliant broadcaster Monty Modlyn, asking him, if I could get Bill Cotton to change his mind, would he be interested in presenting the programme. He said he would. I had been so impressed by Monty's ability in front of the camera. I saw once an interview he did at the stately home of a couple called Lord and Lady Masserene and Ferrard. Monty made use of this cumbersome title and employed it repeatedly every time he asked the couple a question,

"Tell me, Lord Masserene and Ferrard and Lady Masserene and Ferrard, how long have there been Lords Masserene and Ferrard in this beautiful stately home?"

Somehow it was obsequious and cheeky at the same time. It was funny and clever. Monty Modlyn also famously interviewed Idi Amin, the mad dictator of Uganda. Asked about the interview later, Monty said,

"People did express their concern, before I went to Uganda, saying things like, 'He has people castrated, you know', to which I replied, "Well, I haven't been doing much in that department lately. I'll take a chance on it."

Bill Cotton would not listen to my reservations and insisted Savile should be the presenter. If only it had been 'Monty'll Fix It'.

24.

BEGINNING OF THE END

A foreign tourist visiting Leeds on November the 9th, 2011 might have assumed he was witnessing a state funeral. The body had lain in state the night before, a massive, solemn cortège brought the town centre to a standstill. A troop of Royal Marines shouldered a gold plated coffin and bore it into the cathedral. Outside giant television screens relayed the proceedings to the crowds, for whom there was no room in the cathedral.

Our visitor might have wondered whose funeral it was - a prime minister's? a member of the Royal Family's? He would have been wrong; it was Jimmy Savile's.

The Monsignor taking the service told the hundreds of mourners packed inside the cathedral "Sir Jimmy Savile can face eternal life with confidence."

Those of us who had been involved with Savile (as we now had to call him) could not face the remaining days of our earthly lives with as much confidence, because in October 2012 Mark Williams-Thomas created a television documentary revealing 'the other side of Jimmy Savile', in which many sexual accusations against Savile were revealed for the first time. I found it strange that I, the man who produced Savile's television shows for twenty-one years, was not consulted as part of this programme. I wrote to Williams-Thomas, asking why he had decided not to interview me. I received no reply.

When after his death, the full horror of Jimmy Savile's paedophilia was revealed, it came as a terrible shock and things got worse, when the papers and the social media started to look for someone to 'blame'. Let's start with the man who produced his television shows for twenty years. The general message seemed to be that people who worked with Savile must have known what was going on and they must have turned a blind eye. Liz Dux from a firm of solicitors, who made £16,000 out of each complainant about Savile's behaviour, said,

"They went there ('Jim'll Fix It) for the experience of their lives and they came away scarred for life."

All of them, Liz? It is strange that I never witnessed any of this scarring, but I feel that anything I say about it sounds as if I am trying to defend Savile's ghastly crimes. Liz Dux shed a lot of crocodile tears on behalf of his victims, while the compensation money rolled in. Dux went on to say that the alleged victims were not motivated by money. She did not say if the same applied to the lawyers dealing with the affair. If there was any money left over after Slater and Gordon's considerable costs, it went to the victims. The same firm now concentrates on ambulance chasing. "Have you had an injury at work?" asks their advertising, and would probably like to add. "No? No injuries at work? Go on think about it. There must have been something!" I cannot help thinking that they had not the slightest concern about the victims' suffering and were interested only in how many legal fees would accrue.

I managed to speak to Liz Dux and asked her if she could – without saying any names – tell me how many of our two thousand 'fixees' had claimed to have been assaulted on the premises of the 'Jim'll Fix It' studio. She replied that it would be 'most inappropriate' to tell me. I guessed I would never know.

Soon after the ghastly revelations started to emerge, I appeared on 'Good Morning' to be lightly grilled by Philip Schofield and Holly Willoughby. I honestly stated my ignorance of Savile's misdeeds. Daisy McAndrew, the broadcaster, was on the same programme and declared that she was fed up with hearing people like me saying that they did not know. "Didn't want to know, more likely," she added with a sarcastic smile.

Interestingly, McAndrew, was once press secretary to the Liberal Democrat Leader, Charles Kennedy. During that time she came into close contact with Christopher Rennard, the liberal peer, also known after allegations of sexual harassment as 'Lord Grope'. When those allegations were revealed, McAndrew sprang to Rennard's defence, saying that she knew nothing of his alleged importuning.

"Or didn't want to know?", I longed to cry, but, in fact, I think Daisy McAndrew genuinely did not know. Like me she had been fooled by a cunning and secretive man.

The pattern for the recording days was that Savile would arrive at the studio at lunchtime. We had already rehearsed everything else in the programme that did not concern him, such as the pop music items. Jim's dressing room door was always open, to receive visits from me, the researchers, make-up, wardrobe and visiting journalists. Savile may have made some of his evil assignations on the premises, but I could see how he could have carried them out there. Immediately after the recordings a taxi would arrive to take him to his London flat, Stoke Mandeville hospital or Broadmoor where he could get up to whatever he got up to, but in the studio I cannot believe there was time for his paedophilia.

Many people became very wise after the event. Bill Oddie is on record as saying "Everybody knew about Jimmy Savile". He does not seem quite clear on what it was that 'everybody knew' but, if Bill Oddie knew the full horror of what was going on, I wish he had told me. He seemed happy enough to appear on 'Jim'll Fix It' at the time and never said a word to me about it. Did the 'everybody' include the government Honours Committee, who made Savile a knight and the Vatican, who gave him a papal knighthood? Was Mrs Thatcher a member of the 'everybody', when she invited him to spend Christmas at Chequers? Or the Prince of Wales and his wife, who frequently entertained him? Even the very astute Louis Theroux, who examined the man over a period of months, was fooled. To quote his new book, 'Got to Get Theroux This', speaking of rumours about Savile, Louis says:

"Naturally one assumed that, if he had been a paedophile or a necrophile, then forty years plus in the spotlight of British entertainment would have brought something solid to light".

So, apart from 'everybody', Bill, it seems there were quite a few people who – like me - did not know. It is very easy to 'know' things with the benefit of hindsight, but hindsight is available only to the accusers - not the accused. The implication continued that we at the BBC all knew what he was doing, but turned a blind eye to it. At any rate, that is the reaction I got now from the social media and people I talked to. Savile was a very clever and cunning man and it appears he was highly skilled at covering his tracks. I imagine he was obsessed by his paedophilia and would do everything in his power to avoid detection. He probably got an extra kick from the fact that he might have had tea at Clarence House or Number Ten, Downing Street before going on to prowl 'his' hospitals that same night.

There is a saying in French, *'On ne peut pas pendre des squelettes'*, you cannot hang skeletons. For want of a skeleton, it became necessary for the government, press and social media to find somebody else to blame for Savile's misdeeds. Something also had to be seen to be done. What better than an inquiry? It allows the government to say, "We are doing something about it" and then wash their hands of the matter. The effectiveness of inquiries was beautifully summed up in the ever brilliant 'Yes, Minister' (written by Jonathan Lynn and Anthony Jay).

Sir Humphrey tells Jim Hacker, "A basic rule of government is, never look into anything you don't have to, and never set up an inquiry unless you know in advance what its findings will be."

To which Jim Hacker replies, "I don't want an enquiry; I want to know what happened."

So, what was the result of these two and a half years of investigations? Not much. We know you cannot hang skeletons. So what was it all for? Will there be new laws designed to stop such things happening in the future? Existing anti child-abuse legislation seems to miss the mark in the most clumsy ways. For example, it is forbidden for a wedding photographer to take pictures of a choir, if any of the choristers are under sixteen. If present legislation forbids pictures of a church choir in their cassocks, future rulings will have a job to be even more crass and pointless than that. New laws will simply create more bureaucracy and there will always be clever, evil people, who will find a way round any legislation, while the lives of the innocent majority will be encumbered with yet more red tape. The only tangible results of the enquiry were some very rich lawyers and some millions of pounds less for the BBC to spend on programmes.

Hindsight would be a wonderful gift. I wonder if Ronnie Biggs's employers knew that he was planning the Great Train Robbery? Probably not. I imagine Ronnie Biggs kept it a secret. Rather dramatically the victims of Savile's crimes were referred to BBC Director General, Tony Hall, as 'survivors'. However awful he was, I do not think Savile ever actually murdered anyone, although I do remember him saying that he would have liked to be the official hangman.

One can only guess at what the Dame Janet Smith enquiry must have cost. Reed Smith, the solicitors handling the inquiry, are not a company that any money-conscious individuals would approach to handle their affairs. Their vast offices are in the most expensive part of the City of London. The reception area alone is big enough for a game of squash. At £700 annual rent and rates per square yard, that is quite a cost to be covered, before you start hiring a boardroom, a High Court judge, two top barristers and an array of legal secretaries every working day for two and a half years. Reed Smith is employed by people spending corporate money – not their own.

In the Dame Janet Smith enquiry I and others in a similar position were asked if we 'ought to have known' about Savile. Now, there's a difficult concept: 'ought to have known'. Ought I to have known the winner of the 1977 Grand National (Red Rum, his third victory)? Ought the fellow crew members of Andreas Lübitz to have known that he was going to fly their plane into a mountain? It would certainly have been to their advantage, if they had. I wish I had known what Jimmy Savile was up to. I could have done something about it. However, I should be happy that Dame Janet in her report declared me to be genuinely ignorant of Savile's misdeeds, but a little naïve. I'll buy that.

What was the psychology that made Savile behave the way he did? He was almost certainly a psychopath, 'a person suffering from a chronic mental disorder and displaying abnormal social behaviour'. I went on record as saying that I probably knew him as well as anybody did, but that - like the others - I did not know him well at all. He was - understandably – very secretive. If he was being interviewed by a show business reporter, whose only intention was to give the programme a glowing report, he would usually treat the interview as if it were a police inquiry, dodging the questions altogether or giving an evasive answer. On other occasions he would give boastful replies, suggesting great sexual prowess or hinting that he used Mafioso tactics, when he managed his club in Manchester. I believed that this bluster was all self aggrandisement and braggadocio, and wondered if he was actually asexual. I suggested to him once that, as presenter of a youth-orientated programme, he ought not to go into print, saying such questionable things. His response to that was, "If I had listened to advice all my life from people like you, I would not be where I am today."

Was he himself abused as a child? It is said that those circumstances can make someone an abuser. Was his attitude, "this is what sex is. It's what you do"? He was obsessed with his mother and never spoke a word about his father. Maybe his father abused him. One of Savile's brothers, Johnny, who traded on his brother's fame and who also worked in hospitals, was once dismissed from a hospital job due to 'gross misconduct'. After Jimmy Savile's death, further accusations arose about Johnny Savile's sexual misbehaviour. John died several years before Jimmy but the fact that he had acted in the same way as his famous brother suggests that there might have been an inherited pattern of abuse in the Savile family. Since Savile's death a horrifying number of revelations of improper sexual behaviour by people in high places has come to light – even a Roman Catholic archbishop. That does not exonerate Savile in any way, but seems to make his activities less rare than we might previously have hoped.

'Jim'll Fix It' was my baby and its huge success thrilled me. Now the programme has disappeared. It has been airbrushed from the BBC's Kremlin balcony. If there is a list called, for instance, 'Top TV Shows from the 80s', the programme is not on that list, despite the fact that on several occasions 'Jim'll Fix It' was first in the weekly list of audience sizes, the combined list of BBC and ITV, meaning that the show had more viewers than 'Coronation Street' and 'This is Your Life'. However, it is not there. It never existed.

But I refuse to let that fact make me also have to erase all my personal memories of 'Jim'll Fix It'. Jimmy Savile had virtually nothing to do with the programme that bore his name. When he arrived in the studio on recording days, he would ask me, "What have I fixed today?" The team devised it, selected the requests, pursued and realised them. It was a great job with a wonderful, creative team. Unfortunately unbeknown to us, the presenter was a villain. Ironically the programme received Mary Whitehouse's national Viewers and Listeners' Association annual award, which we rather reluctantly accepted in 1976.

On a lighter, note Savile once asked me to speak to one of Broadmoor hospital's directors, suggesting events that might be possible for what they remarkably called an 'Open Day'. The director told me that on a previous Open Day they had included

Crazy Golf, but he added that they did not call it 'Crazy Golf'. It was considerately renamed it 'Hazard Golf'. I went to the 'Open Day', which was , as you can imagine, not all that open. Savile said to me beforehand, "Remember, every hand you shake has been round someone's throat".

While, where possible, I avoid reference to the man, whose unspeakable name the programme bore, please bear with me, as I mention some of the remarkable times we had putting these programmes together. Programmes, which, I like to think, gave a great deal of pleasure to audiences of up to twenty million people at a time and the making of which did not involve Savile other than as a front man.

25.

FIXTURES AND FITTINGS

Most organisations were willing to help us, if only because of the positive publicity they hoped involvement with the programme would supply. Those who did not wish to help usually gave one of the following replies:

a. We should love to do this but unfortunately our insurance does not allow us to.
b. If we let one person do it, they'd all want to.

Let me give you an example of (b), which happened within the BBC's own Television Centre. Back in 1975, as they do now, the Corporation used the working newsroom as a background for the newsreader. It was more clearly visible then than it is now and you could see working news folk at their desks behind the reader, answering phones and typing reports. Occasionally a busy messenger could be seen scurrying across the office with a news story freshly torn from the teleprinter. All old stuff now, but as far as Gwen Charlton from Morpeth, Northumberland, was concerned, all this activity was much more interesting than the news itself and she hit upon a most original idea. She wanted to ride a white horse through the back of the news room, while Richard Baker was reading the news.

We could not, of course, do that during the actual news, but Richard Baker agreed to read some special news items just for our programme, perhaps what we would now call 'fake news'. The man in charge of BBC TV News, like me, lived in Richmond. I would occasionally see him going in to work on the tube and took one of those opportunities to ask him his permission. The idea amused him and he gave his assent. The trouble was that the news room was on the sixth floor of the Television Centre and the house manager of TV Centre, the man responsible for the bricks and mortar of the building, was a 'no' man (One met them more frequently than 'yes' men). "The weight of a horse's hoof per square inch would exceed the safety loading limit of my floors," he said. I thought I already knew people working at the BBC, who weighed more than a small horse, but offered to have boards laid down to spread the load.

"What if the horse makes a mess on my floors?"

I offered to have tarpaulins laid and to clean up any muck myself. For a moment he was cornered but then he remembered standard reply (b).

"If I let you do it, they'll all want to do it,."

"No they won't, David!", I replied vociferously. I think in his troubled mind he was picturing hordes of zebras, camels and rhinoceroses all queuing to get into his nice, clean newsroom. However, I have to say in the house manager's favour that he did at last give in and we were able to stage our own little news story. "People are looking for Gwen Charlton of Morpeth, Northumberland," announced Richard Baker, " She was last seen riding a white horse in the region of the BBC's Television Centre in London" Enter Gwen weaving her way between the desks on 'Snowball'. The effect was delightful.

I managed to obtain from the Distiller's Company a large poster advertising a whisky with the slogan that was well known at the time. I sent it to the house manager's office. It said, "You can take a White Horse anywhere."

Filming for our first Christmas transmission, we were in Bethlehem with an Israeli crew, trying to take a peaceful shot to establish the exterior of the Church of the Nativity, the oldest site continuously used as a place of worship in Christianity. Our 'fixee' and a priest were walking through Manger Square towards the church. Manger Square is quite a busy thoroughfare and the noisy traffic was spoiling the tranquillity we had been hoping for. Just as the fifth take was coming to a successful end, a large American convertible came hurtling down the road, blaring its horn. Trying to imitate Sylvester the cat, I shouted "Aaah Shuddup!" at no-one in particular. There was a screech of brakes and a portly Arab gentlemen leapt out of the car and walked towards us.

"Who say 'Shut up'?" he demanded. I stepped forward. "It was me," I replied and, trying to avoid the start of World War Three, added rather unconvincingly, "but I was talking to the cameraman."

The Arab gentleman's eyes narrowed. "No!", he insisted. "It is not to him you say 'Shut up'; it is to me you say 'Shut up'."

I looked sheepish. The Arab gentleman took a deep breath and said:

"To me you say 'Shut up'. To you I say..."

There was a pause. I was waiting for one of those spectacular Arab curses involving dogs and my family. The Arab gentleman continued, his eyes narrowing:

"To me you say, 'Shut up'. To you I say, 'One hundred shut ups!'".

He turned on his heel and strode back to his car. The incident was closed. We re-named Manger Square 'The Street of the One Hundred Shut Ups'.

In a more peaceful environment we were doing a 'recce' the day before filming in a steeply sloping tea plantation in beautiful Sri Lanka. As nearly always, we used a local crew. Many of the young women tea-pickers were extremely beautiful and therefore very photogenic for the following day's shoot. Due to a poor diet, or perhaps too much tea, a lot of the older women had lost some of their teeth. In my mind I was preparing a rather delicate and probably sexist question that I wanted to put to the plantation manager. Could the next day's filming feature only the younger women? In the manager's office I took a deep breath and said, "Mr Gunawardena, I was wondering if tomorrow, when we are filming, it might perhaps be possible, if the camera were to concentrate on, how shall I put it?, the younger women, er...What I mean is...er..."

FIXTURES AND FITTINGS

The manager held up his hands, "Say no more, Mr Ordish. I understand completely. Leave it to me."

He seized a phone from the desk in front of him and barked into it,

"Mr. Samarasinghe, for the filming tomorrow, only beautiful pluckers. Understood?"

"Thank you, Mr Gunawardena," I mumbled.

So, beautiful pluckers it was to be. The crew, who arrived the following day, was about seven men strong and it soon emerged that the cameraman and the sound recordist were the officers and the rest were 'the men'. The camera, a lend-lease donation from Hollywood apparently, was very heavy and used 35 millimetre film, which I had never worked with before. There were large metal reflectors for lighting close-up shots, which had to be carried up and down the precipitous slopes of the plantation. At one point the cameraman decided that the crew were not working fast enough. He clapped his hands and shouted something to them in Sinhala (or was it Tamil?). They started running. Thinking of our unionised crews, I commented, "We don't do it quite like that in Ealing."

I got back to Heathrow with a dozen or so cans of exposed 35mm film. To open a can of exposed celluloid in daylight would ruin the film, but a can of film might also contain heroin or blood diamonds. It was therefore a very delicate operation, taking exposed film through customs. The BBC employed a specialist, Pat Furlong, himself a former customs and excise man. But there was no Pat at the airport. What was I to do? I knocked at a door marked 'Customs and Excise'. Hearing a "Come in", I entered the room to see six or seven customs officers lounging round a table with cups of tea. I explained my predicament and, looking at the telephone on their table, asked if it would be possible for me to call the B.B.C.

"There's a phone box out there," replied a nasty looking, little man, pointing to the other side of the customs area.

"But would I not need to go through customs to get to the phone box?" I asked.

"You can leave the film cans here, while you go through customs." snapped little Mr. Nasty.

"Unfortunately I have not got any English money for the phone box," I explained.

"There's a bank out there as well," I was told with evident satisfaction.

After a ten hour flight I felt myself at the end of my tether. I looked at these little Hitlers lounging round their table, doing nothing and said foolishly:

"Well. I apologise for having interrupted you, when you are clearly so busy."

That was it for Hitler Junior. He got up from the table and, rising to his full five foot one, glared up at me. I don't remember all of what he said but he kept slapping the palm of his hand with one of those leather tabs on the end of a chain, while he lectured me on the arduous duties of customs men.

"There are more important things in the world than the B.B.C.," was one of his lines that stuck in my mind.

I smiled weakly and agreed. In the end I was rescued, when Pat Furlong, our import expert, did arrive and saved the day. Pat somehow proved that I was not importing cocaine or blood diamonds. I am sure you will understand why I have always maintained a high regard for the staff of HMCR.

Any broadcast exposure of a commercial product is to some extent advertising it. Public relations people were on to us constantly, offering help from national tourist boards, airlines and hotels. When does informative television become advertising? A delicate balance had to be maintained. I was getting a bit of a reputation as a 'bon viveur', when we had a producers' meeting with Bill Cotton, at which the question of incidental advertising was raised. We had been negotiating to film the Olympic swimmer, David Wilkie, at an event sponsored by the Coca Cola Corporation. I said that I had recently had lunch with Coca Cola. Bill Cotton retorted, "I'm pleased to hear it".

FIXTURES AND FITTINGS

As well as being a brilliant, if confrontational, tennis player, the young John McEnroe was also something of a pin-up and the programme was inundated with requests from female teenagers, to meet him or play tennis with him. Many of his fans were not tennis players but simply youngsters, who admired his style and his cheek, and particularly his frequent outraged complaint to the umpires, "You cannot be serious!" There were hundreds of letters to choose from, all from females, some of whom were competent players, requesting a game, but I felt that a fairly good player being defeated by John McEnroe would not make interesting television and decided to select instead a couple of non-playing girl fans. John agreed to take part in the programme while he was training at the Bisham Abbey National Sports Centre on the Thames near Marlow.

Although they could not play tennis, we kitted the girls out in Wimbledon-style whites and I went to speak to McEnroe in his dressing room. I could hear from outside the room that he was on the telephone but I knocked anyway and received a gruff 'Come in!'. He was in the middle of a furious argument with somebody on the phone - maybe it was with his agent about what we were about to do. When he finally rang off, he turned to me and said,

"I suppose you think I'm some kind of an asshole!"

"That's not for me to say, Mr. McEnroe," I replied.

He could not understand why I had chosen two girls, who could not play tennis. I explained that they were huge fans of his and that this would be their first lesson. Eventually he recovered from his grumpiness and entered into the spirit of the thing, saying in exasperation at their ineptitude "If you do not return this ball to me, I shall throw you both into the river Thames!". He pronounced the river's name as it is spelt 'Thaymes' to rhyme with 'games'. Since we were right next to the gently flowing river, I seized the opportunity to bring the film to a positive finish. I asked the girls and John McEnroe if they would be happy for this threat to be carried out. Everyone agreed and John pushed these two good sports from a gently sloping muddy bank into the edge of the river. I am sure they could not wait to get back to school and say, "Guess what! Yesterday John McEnroe threw us in the river!"

The vast majority of three hundred and fifty thousand requests sent to the programme each year were repetitive and dull. Most people wanted to 'meet' a pop star or a footballer, the result of which was likely to make boring viewing. In the dozens of 'oysters' that arrived in our office, we would occasionally find pearls, such as:

"I would like to cook eggs on the shovel in a steam locomotive"

"I get fined if I slam doors at home. Please can I slam a hundred doors somewhere free of charge?"

"My mum says I am worth my weight in gold. How much is my weight in gold worth?".

"My dad says I couldn't fight my way out of a paper bag. I want to prove him wrong."

The programme had not been intended as a children's programme, although that was how it used to be referred to, before it was not referred to any more. Letters from adults would often make me feel, "Well, if that's what you really want to do, why don't you just do it?"

Two female pupils from a school in Barnet wrote, complaining that the music played at morning assembly was usually "Bach and things like that". They wanted something a bit more up to date. We did not respond to these two young women but instead contacted their headmaster, who gave us permission to fulfil the request. At an unearthly hour for pop musicians we managed somehow to smuggle Boy George and his band into the school, before the pupils started to arrive and the musicians were already hiding backstage as the boys and girls started filing into assembly. The headmaster addressed the school, explaining the presence of the film crew as 'part of an educational documentary'. He went on to say that the staff were always keen to hear constructive suggestions from the pupils and then read out the letter that had been sent to the programme. The camera recorded the letter-writers' shock as they heard their words read out. A curtain behind the headmaster was drawn back and to the school's delight Boy George launched into his hit song 'Karma Chameleon'. We did not transmit Boy George's final words to the school assembly, "Right, now I want all the boys and girls to swap uniforms…"

Another school surprise was the result of a very original letter from the Treloar School for the disabled near Alton, Hampshire, which said, "Our school is near an army air station. When the helicopters fly low over our classroom, our French teacher, Mr. Terry, pretends to be the air traffic controller and talks into his pen as if it was a microphone and he is speaking to the pilot. Could you fix it for a helicopter really to land and collect Mr. Terry?"

I decided that would not really work but I wondered if, as with the Boy George surprise, we could turn the request round and, instead of surprising Mr. Terry, we could surprise the French class. The school gave us the go-ahead. The Army Air Corps agreed to do it and Mr. Terry was happy to play his key role. We asked for total secrecy to be maintained and once again the pupils were told that a BBC crew would be filming for a forthcoming documentary programme.

Right on cue a helicopter started flying low over the school and Mr. Terry began to talk into his pen. "Ah, good, you're there. Could you come and collect me now, please?" the class were laughing and the laughter turned into gasps as the helicopter landed on the playing field outside the ground floor classroom. The pilot entered the room. "Good morning, Mr. Terry," he said, "As you requested, I have come to collect you." And that is what he did. The children loved it and a very moving shot was the entire class exiting the class, whatever their disabilities, and cheering their very popular French master, as he took off into the wild, blue yonder. It was one of the happiest occasions we recorded for the programme. However, having done some Google research on this event just now, I was horrified to learn that at the recording of this programme, Savile somehow secretly groped one of the disabled pupils actually in the studio with everyone there. She is Julie Fernandez, who is now an actress and has appeared regularly on television in 'The Office' and other programmes. That is the first evidence I have learnt of Savile's misconduct on my watch. I am disgusted. God, how I hate the man!

Savile has cast shame on the event, but that piece of filming before he was involved with it in any way remains innocently delightful. Thank God he did not come filming with us.

The first item in the first programme was of a young woman, who wanted to swim with a dolphin. The delight on her face, when the dolphin swam up to her, changed her whole appearance. With an expression of total delight she grabbed the dolphin's fin and launched into the pool. It was tear-jerking in a happy way, which was one of our objectives with the programme. Sometimes we succeeded.

The programme did give us an opportunity to 'see the world', but usually only briefly. I went to Sydney, Australia and Alice Springs, for example, but was back in the office in London after less than a week's absence.

14 year old Catriona Nisbett's letter was a tall order. She wanted to be 'an ambassador for a day'. I did not expect a positive response from the Foreign Office but, when I spoke to their press officer, he took me seriously and was most helpful. At our preliminary discussion we said we wanted Catriona to have the toughest assignment that they would allow and asked if Moscow might be a possible placement for our young ambassador. This was in 1985 before the start of the East-West thaw and it was asking a lot. However, our man in Moscow, Sir Bryan Cartledge, was approached and he gave an OK, as far as he was concerned. Our request to pursue the project went right up the line to the Foreign Secretary, Sir Geoffrey Howe. He not only gave his assent but said that, when Catriona came back from her posting, she should follow

the correct ambassadorial procedure and make a report to him personally. We would film the debriefing. For reasons of economy, when we filmed overseas, we usually worked with a local film crew. I made the mistake of asking if it would be possible for us to us to work with a Soviet crew while we were in Moscow and got the reply, "Are you mad? A Russian film crew in the British Embassy? They'd love that and we're certainly not going to fix it for them!"

We had the go-ahead from the Foreign Office, but there was still the hurdle of getting approval from Moscow to be cleared. The authorities there were very dubious about what we were up to, suspecting, I think, that we would be trying to disseminate anti-Soviet propaganda. It was hard enough trying to explain to them what the programme was about. There was no 'Alexei Will Fix It' on Soviet television. The phone calls which researcher, Jeremy Geelan, made, sorting out the details, must have added up to a week of phone-time. With an enormous amount of help from the British Embassy and the BBC's man in Moscow we were finally given permission to film. One week later a new problem arose. The British government decided to expel some senior Soviet diplomats on charges of spying. As always, Moscow immediately reciprocated by repatriating the same number of British diplomats in what the papers called a 'tit-for-tat' expulsion. Our Moscow embassy was therefore understaffed and in no mood for unnecessary activity. The project for the time being was cancelled. The following year with a slightly improved diplomatic climate we started all over again and this time we were successful. The Soviet authorities took us much more seriously than they needed to. A KGB 'heavy', whom we called 'Comrade Niet', accompanied us everywhere and I know that our telephones were bugged. The people at our embassy, including a Scottish aristocrat called 'the Maclean of Maclean', did a great job. Our ambassador, Sir Bryan, graciously made himself scarce. "While Catriona is here, she is the ambassador," he said. "She may have the use of my Rolls Royce and the car may fly my Union Flag." (Only the ambassador is normally allowed to do that.) The members of 'her' staff stood up respectfully, when Catriona entered the room for a meeting and delivered their reports to her exactly as they would to the real ambassador. Her gleaming, chauffeur-driven Rolls stood out like an extremely elegant thumb among the Ladas, as she drove past the Kremlin on her way to visit a political reception at the Orwellian-sounding 'House of Friendship', a British Trade Fair, a rather surprising pop concert given by the Nolan Sisters and a one-to-one meeting with the American ambassador in his embassy. One of my favourite 'double-takes' was that done by the Russian soldier on guard outside the United States embassy. As the ambassadorial Roller rolled into the embassy driveway, he sprang to attention and 'presented' his Kalashnikov rifle in salute. He then looked into the car and saw, not the British ambassador, but a fourteen-year-old young woman, looking as cool as a cucumber and giving him a regal nod. Our final bit of filming was in London, when our temporary ambassador in Moscow reported to Sir Geoffrey Howe at the Foreign Office.

26.

MRS THATCHER

We went one better than the Foreign Secretary, by securing two filming dates with Margaret Thatcher. The first was in 1977, when she was famously the first ever female Leader of the Opposition. Four youngsters interviewed her in her office in the Houses of Parliament. Ten years later we invited the same children to meet Mrs. T. again, this time as Prime Minister. As was only right, one of them declined the offer on political grounds, but then she was at university.

Margaret Thatcher was at the height of her success and confidence on this second occasion and I have to say, she was pretty impressive. I was introduced to her and she said, "What would you like me to do?" I suppose I could have replied, "Stop privatising monopolies," But I didn't.

After the cameras had finished rolling and to no advantage to herself as publicity, Mrs Thatcher showed us all round Number Ten in some detail. She complained that the 'Fix-it' badges had red ribbons and suggested that a Tory blue would be much more appropriate. We made up a badge for her with a blue ribbon, for which I got into trouble on grounds of political bias. At least after that she cannot have thought that I was a 'Pinko'.

In making the programme we had to be very careful not to do anything really dangerous. Every activity involves some degree of danger but I believed we should not take a risk any greater than that of driving a car on a public road. We had some fun doing things that looked fairly dangerous, as was the case with a young woman, who wanted to stand on an aircraft's wing in mid-air. Breathtaking and alarming it certainly looked, but since she was securely strapped on, she was as safe on the wing, as she would have been sitting in the seat next to the pilot.

In the summer of 1981 inhabitants of St Ives, Cornwall, who are not easily surprised, raised their eyebrows, when they saw a bright red Ford Cortina hurtle along their jetty and go straight off the end and into the sea. A young mother of no fewer than five, Hillary Nichols, was looking for a challenge other than that of looking after five young children. She decided that nothing would suit her better than driving off the end of a pier. Was it dangerous? Not unreasonably so. The safety precautions for the exercise were stringent. Stunt director, Tim Condren, was in charge of the operation and he first supervised the drilling of holes in the old banger we had bought for the job (later to be re-sold for scrap). The purpose of the holes, Tim explained, was to make the car sink as quickly as possible. The behaviour of a car which goes straight under is more predictable than that of a near-watertight vehicle bobbing about on the surface for a few minutes. Ballast was added to the vehicle to encourage it to nose-dive, rather than make a spiralling entry into the sea. Tim tested Hillary's ability to swim under water and gave her lessons in using the breathing apparatus at the depth she would reach, when the car hit the bottom. He explained that he would be in the car sitting next to her, when we filmed. Aircraft-style safety harnesses were attached to the seats. Hillary had a test drive on dry land and then she was ready to go. Tim gave a signal to his two stuntmen/divers, who dropped off the end of the jetty to be on standby under the water, in case any unforeseen problem should arise. Two cameras were ready to film the event, one at the end of the jetty and the other on the inshore lifeboat, kindly lent to us for the occasion. There was a big crowd of onlookers and it was well known that we would be doing the stunt at five minutes to four, at which time the tide would be at its optimum height. Then there was a snag. At six minutes to four an anonymous and mentally-deranged person, presumably with a grudge against us or against the world in general, made a hoax distress call for the lifeboat. Our waterborne film crew had to evacuate the lifeboat as quickly as possible and luckily a neighbouring fisherman generously loaned us his fishing vessel as a substitute, but, due to the hoax call we were running a few minutes late for the most suitable height of tide and maybe that is why things did not go exactly as planned. On the other hand it could have been that Hillary drove the car a little bit faster than she had been told to. The Cortina hit the water square-on and started to sink quickly as planned, but, once under water, it slowly continued its forward roll and in the end landed upside down on the bottom. Tim Condren, now also upside down in the passenger seat, could still just see his driver despite the murky water. She had correctly inserted the breathing apparatus in her mouth, she had undone her safety harness and was calmly feeling for the door handle. To us on the jetty it felt like an age before the driver and passenger rose to the surface again. In fact there had been only thirty-seven seconds between the car hitting the water and the re-emergence of Hillary and Tim. Hilary snatched the breathing tube out of her mouth and shouted, "Can we do it again, please?"

(Safety foot note: A large crane immediately fished the crumpled car back out of the sea.)

I took a train to Liverpool for a meeting with Ken Dodd about filming his 'Diddy Men'. Ken met me at Lime Street station and drove me in his van to Knotty Ash, which until then I thought was a place he had invented. During the drive Ken asked me, "How are you, Roger?", to which I replied, "Not at my best, Ken. My wife has just left me," which she had. Ken pondered for a moment and said.

"We have a saying here in Liverpool, Roger: 'An empty house is better than an unwanted tenant'."

"I suppose you are right, Ken," I replied, "Thank you for that." Ken then added.

"Mind you, we normally say that after someone has farted."

The appropriately named Pamela Hailstone wanted to build an igloo. When it snowed in her home town of Morpeth,

Northumberland, to use an expression made famous later by British Rail, it was 'the wrong kind of snow'. It would not stick together properly and, if Pamela ever got as far as trying to make a ceiling, it would collapse immediately. Igloos are part of the culture only amongst the Innuit people of Northern Canada and Alaska. It would have been prohibitively expensive to travel to such territories, but we did discover that at the university of Greenland there was a course of Inuit studies, where researchers were investigating amongst other things how igloos were made. We could get to Greenland on our budget and with the help of the Danish Tourist Board, set off to film there. Not surprisingly it was extremely cold but we were kitted out for the job. The last part of our journey was by dog-drawn sledge. The days were very long in that part of the world at that time of year and we got our igloo built with time to spare. Unlike Pamela's Northumbrian slush, the Greenland snow was very light and crisp. It was easy to pick up a brick the size of a breeze block and the bricks cemented themselves naturally to each other by the slight melting and refreezing of the ice on its edges.

We filmed a ship launch in Hamburg, where with German efficiency the champagne bottle was placed in a net bag for health and safety reasons. The result was that the bottle would not break against the ship's bow. There were five failed naming ceremonies, before the safety bag had to be abandoned. On another occasion we created a mock ceremony for a young man, who had been born outside Yorkshire, but hoped one day to play cricket for that county. You cannot play cricket for Yorkshire, if you were not born there. Could he become a naturalised Yorkshireman? One of his tests was having to understand phrases like 'apastate in't mornin' (half past eight in the morning).

Two veterans who had taken part in the D-Day landings wanted to re-enact the experience. I guess they were in their sixties, but travelled with us from Portsmouth to Arromanches on a choppy sea in a bobbing landing-craft and jumped in full kit into the icy water on the French side. There were no machine guns, trying to kill them this time, but the Mayor of Arromanches was waiting for them on the beach as they waded ashore. He gave them both a Gallic hug. Safer than bullets but terribly embarrassing.

We filmed the latest James Bond car at the old Brooklands racing circuit and airfield where we tried to recreate a Bond car chase. A man approached me and said, "I've seen that film. Wasn't James Bond's car also being chased by a helicopter?" I replied, "Yes, but we can't afford a helicopter." The man said, "I'll lend you mine. Hop in and tell me where you would like me to fly." Nervously I climbed into his tiny aircraft and said, "You see where the camera is. Try to keep the helicopter in shot, either on the other side of the car or between the car and the camera." It was hair-raising but the finished product looked great.

One fix-it, which led to a bit of a kerfuffle, was a request from a boy named Toby, that he should have a Toby Jug made in his likeness. We approached Royal Doulton of Stoke-on-Trent, who were delighted at the prospect of the publicity that such an item would create. We took Toby to the factory and filmed him sitting for his ceramic likeness and then watching the manufacturing process right through to the finished, painted jug. On the studio day, when the film was shown, the representative of Royal Doulton announced to viewers, that, after the mould for the jug had been made, only three jugs had been manufactured and then they had literally broken the mould. One of the jugs was for the boy, Toby, another was for the company museum and the third one was to be sold at auction for charity. We filmed the sale at Sotheby's in London, that included the jug. To our surprise the item fetched £16,000. The bad news for young Toby was that, on hearing the sum it had raised, his parents put his jug up for auction as well, where I assume it fetched a similar price. This caused a bit of a stir at the BBC, where it was decreed that henceforth, if, as a result of the programme, an object of value was acquired by the 'fixee', he or she would become the object's 'tenant for life' rather than its owner. That meant the owner could not sell the object.

A similar situation arose a few years later. A mother had seen Thomas Lawrence's famous portrait of a young girl, known as 'Pinkie', on one of a series of recently issued postage stamps. The mother's request was that a copy of the painting should be made, featuring her daughter's face rather than that of the original young girl. A brilliant copyist (possibly a brilliant forger) was booked to paint the portrait and the result was amazingly good. I rang the mother some time after the transmission to explain about the 'tenant for life' clause. "You can have the painting permanently," I told her, "but you cannot sell it." She was furious. Whether she had really wanted to sell the painting, or was insulted by the suggestion that she might want to sell it, I am not sure, but she would have nothing more to do with Pinkie. Therefore, incongruously, the elegant painting in its elaborate gilt frame hung for several years in our grim 1960s office in Shepherds Bush. When I left the BBC, the lovely Jenny Ricotti, who had been one of the researchers on 'Fix It' suggested that I should take the unclaimed and unwanted picture home with me and get a portrait painter to insert my daughter Lulu's face by painting over the existing face, which is what we did. Now I have a lovely full-size portrait of my beautiful daughter as 'Pinkie'. (*illustration 'Pinkie'*)

There was a ten year old girl who wanted to be a beautician for a day. We filmed at a health farm and the beautiful singer, Kim Wilde, agreed to be the person being pampered (the 'pamperee', perhaps). We had filmed a wide shot of some talcum powder being applied to Kim Wilde's bare feet and I decided that we should take a close-up of the same thing. Kim's feet were already covered with talcum powder, which for purposes of 'continuity' had to be removed for the re-take. I huffed and puffed and blew the powder off her feet.

"What were you doing at work today, darling?" I was asked. "I was blowing talcum powder off Kim Wilde's feet."

27.

SPECTRA

Social science provides us with many spectrums (spectra?) today. I took part recently in a television programme entitled, 'Meet the Psychopaths', not because I am one, but because the producer wanted a discussion about Jimmy Savile, who was rated by the programme as fairly high on the psychopathic spectrum. Is there an eccentricity spectrum? If there is, we must all be somewhere on it. No-one is completely normal, surely. To my mind a real eccentric does not consider himself or herself different from the rest of us. My favourite eccentric at the BBC was Tom Corcoran, a very clever electronic physicist, who found himself directing a pop music programme known as the 'Old Grey Whistle Test', an obscure title referring to a test that record producers used to try to assess the memorability of a piece of music. 'Whistle' is rhyming slang for 'suit' (whistle and flute). If a doorman in his grey suit could hum the tune after hearing a recording once or twice, the product might be a success. I digress. We were talking about Tom Corcoran and eccentricity. I was briefly his tenant in Barnes, West London and, while my room was reasonably clean and tidy, the rest of the house was a bit of a jumble and the garden was as wild as nearby Barnes Common. My girlfriend at the time was Ruth Pearson, a member of 'Pan's People', a six girl dance group, who appeared weekly on 'Top of the Pops' and whom Jonathan Ross described as the reason for his poor eyesight. Ruth and I decided that we would like to learn the tango and told Tom of our ambition. Returning to my room in his house one evening, I discovered that Tom had somehow painted on to the ceiling beautifully drawn footsteps, indicating 'right' foot' and 'left foot' and numbered to show the progression of a tango. The accompanying literature stated: 'Doctor Corcoran's sleep induction method. Learn to dance while you slumber'. The footsteps on the ceiling actually led to the window, from where, I suppose the dancers would fall into the garden.

Pan's People didn't have WAGS (wives and girlfriends) but I suppose we could have been be called HABS, husbands and boyfriends. In their summer break of 1973 Pan's People and their HABS all went on holiday to Saint Tropez in the South of France. It was the beginning of 'topless' and the girls agreed that they would all remove their bikini tops at the same time, 'One, two, three, OFF!" the HABS tried to look cool and not stare at the revelations. One of the HABS was well-heeled and had hired a Riva speedboat big enough to take us all. One morning we were chugging round St Tropez harbour, getting a close-up look at some of the big yachts moored there. We were admiring a classically shaped vessel, when a man called to us from its deck and, observing Pan's People in what was left of their bikinis, shouted in an English voice: "Why don't you come up for a drink?" We moored and clambered aboard. Our host told a steward to bring a bottle of champagne. The owner shocked me, when he looked at the bottle and said, "No, that's the cheap stuff" throwing the unopened bottle into the sea. The steward returned with several bottles of 'the expensive stuff' and we all toasted Evan Phillips, apparent owner of the vessel. It was all a bit shockingly extravagant. We all stayed on the capacious yacht for three days and nights, visiting Cannes, Nice and Cap d'Antibes. Evan's chauffeur followed the yacht's journey by road in an XK Jaguar, which was lent to Ruth and me one afternoon. I was asked to 'top her up', since the petrol was getting low, to which I readily agreed. We drove into a petrol station but neither Ruth nor I, nor even the pump attendant could find out where the access to the fuel tank was. I am sure the attendant must have thought we had stolen the car. If I remember rightly, we went to a restaurant at Cap d'Antibes, where, after their meal, customers could, if they wished to, throw the furniture they had been sitting on into a bonfire. Who would want to that? Maybe customers who had just seen their bills.

A year or so later we went to visit Evan Phillips in rather different circumstance. He was in prison for tax evasion and supplying pornography.

28.

DE LUXE

The programme did occasionally bring the opportunity of luxury travel as a perk. If only there were a way of flying to places without having to go to an airport. I think Hell is probably an airport. In my BBC work I did a fair amount of flying, sometimes getting a free upgrade to business, or, even better, first class. There is something extra special about flying first class, when you know you could not possibly afford to pay for it. I suppose the owners of private jets turn their noses up at the paupers, who merely fly first class. I did a first class round trip to Sydney and Alice Springs and back, for which the fare would now be over ten thousand pounds. It included a stopover in Hong Kong each way as well, staying at the famous Peninsula Hotel for nothing. On the outward journey my supper started with Krug champagne and my own personal jar of caviar. After the meal I was getting sleepy. It was before the days of beds in first class and for some reason I can only get to sleep, if I am lying face down. Trying to nod off in the massive armchair seat did not work for me but, since I had the very front seat of the whole aircraft, the cabin crew were happy for me to lie face down on blankets and pillows in a makeshift bed on the floor.

It was on one flight in the U.S.A. I heard my two favourite announcements. The pilot informed the passengers that it was 1.30 p.m., then almost immediately came back on the intercom to say that it was actually 3.30 p.m. He then added, "There are so many dials in here, I don't know which is which." Later he announced, "We are flying over Chicago at the moment but you will not be able to see the city, because the sky is undercast." I think I was only in business class that time. Tough. My colleague, Tony James, was flying somewhere on an occasion he told me about. His seat was at the very front of the tourist class section beside the galley, where the business-class meals were prepared. Tony was tucking into his scorching bacon sandwich, when a very camp steward emerged from the galley, pushing a trolley containing a joint of succulent roast beef. He noticed Tony looking at the meat, said, "Jealous?" and swept dramatically through the curtains dividing business and touristclass.

Flying with the R.A.F. was not luxurious but could be very exciting in an alarming way. The subject of one filmed item was air-to-air refuelling, an exercise in which aircraft do something which in any other circumstance they would strenuously avoid. The aircraft have to fly so close to each other, that they touch. The height, the speed and the manoeuvring are all critical. We in the tanker aircraft could see the faces of the fighter pilots as they gave a thumbs-up to indicate that they were successfully connected to the fuel pipe and were taking on kerosene. The services were generally very co-operative and especially loved to do anything out of the ordinary. My colleague and friend, Tony James, was lucky enough to be working with Peter Cook and Dudley Moore in their brilliant 'Not Only, but Also' series. One of the scripts required that during the closing music two dummies at the piano, representing Peter and Dudley, would be fired from an aircraft carrier's steam catapult into the sea. Tony, a brilliant organiser, set the whole thing up with the Royal Navy. At one point during his negotiations for this stunt, he received this signal from H.M.S. Ark Royal:

"'If you require us to fire a piano from the catapult, we suggest that an upright piano be used, since we find that grand pianos tend to break up in mid-air."

There were occasional other perks of the job. We were filming a girl working on a cruise liner, performing as many different jobs as we could fit into the three days that the film crew were with us between Tilbury and Gibraltar. Amongst other tasks, the girl had to be a waitress, a chambermaid and an engineer in the boiler room. No children under a year old were permitted on the cruise.

Our daughter, Lulu, was thirteen months old and just qualified. For a reduced fare she and Susie were allowed to join the cruise, which continued to Mallorca and Barcelona. She became the ship's baby and the Italian waiters loved her. We observed the rituals of cruising, such as what to wear on 'formal', informal' and 'casual' evenings. On a formal evening it was while I was wearing my white dinner jacket that baby Lulu had her first taste of caviar. Her face was smothered in it. I had to carry her at arms' length out of the dining saloon, trying not to get any caviar on my spotless, white tuxedo. An American fellow passenger, whom we christened 'Shelley Winters', would start the day with a couple of Bloody Marys. She was shocked to find that the dress code for one of the evenings had been changed from 'casual' to 'formal'. Shelley had come prepared for only seven formal evenings with a different dress for each of them. Now there were to be eight of them. "Oh, my God," she cried, "I'm gonna have to repeat!"

We flew home from Barcelona and Baby Lulu started to cry, as babies often do during the descent before landing. They cry because their ears hurt due to the change of air pressure in the cabin. We gave Lulu a sip or two of water. The act of swallowing adjusted the pressure in her ears and she stopped crying. I wish airlines would include that as a useful hint in their announcements to passengers.

A perk that money could not buy came as a result of the programme. It was an invitation to have dinner in St James's Palace with a 'Captain of the Guard', who had been involved with the programme. Round the table was a small group of officers from the Scots Guards and the Household Cavalry all resplendent in their dress uniforms. My dinner jacket looked insignificant by comparison. A piper entertained us and royal toasts were drunk. It could have been 1815. Talking of 1815, we fulfilled a request from a young woman to tread grapes. Oporto was recommended as the location, since they really do tread grapes with their feet there and the resulting grape juice is a wonderfully deep colour. As a treat, the manager of the 'quinta' offered us a sip of what they called the

Wellington Port, which they told us, was from the vintage of 1815. I was not sure if I could believe that, but we drank the toast anyway.

There was one unusual request, which I would have enjoyed fulfilling, but was sadly not appropriate.

"My friends say I couldn't organise a piss-up in a brewery. Could you fix it for me to prove them wrong?"

During the productions mentioned above, I was, surprisingly, selected to be an 'ambassador' for the BBC, showing visiting Members of Parliament, including some ministers, round the Television Centre, with the aim of demonstrating to them how cost-conscious and efficient the Corporation was. If they'd believe that, they'd believe anything. It was a very interesting exercise, though. One of my fellow 'ambassadors' was Jane Wellesley, the daughter of the Duke of Wellington, not to be confused with Duke Ellington. Jane Wellesley was famous for once having been Prince Charles's girlfriend. She was then working in the BBC press office. She and I got on very well together and would occasionally have very chaste and innocent lunches at 'La Paesana' restaurant in Notting Hill Gate. All these years later I have just read her excellent book 'Wellington', a history of her family from the Iron Duke to the present day.

As a side line I compiled for a few years an annual connected to the 'Fix-it' programme. Other than those, the only book I have had published was unfortunately on the same theme and entitled "The 'Jim'll Fix It' Story" published by Hodder and Stoughton. If I remember rightly, it sold about a hundred thousand copies and was a nice little earner for me. I was staying with my parents in their Cornish cottage on the day of the book's publication and went to a 'signing' session, appropriately at Waterstone's in Truro. This did not mean there was a queue of eager buyers waiting for me to sign their copies. There was just a pile of the books on a table in the shop, each of which I dutifully signed. I told the delightful young staff in the shop that Tim Waterstone and I had been great friends at school. "Tell us something about him," I was urged. I told them that at a school 'house supper' Tim and I, dressed in little 'flapper' dresses, had mimed to a recording of 'Tiptoe through the Tulips' by the Andrews Sisters. They were suitably amazed.

29.

ENTERTAINMENT

As well as the endless filming for THAT programme, I was allotted other shows to produce. Our production manager in 1986 was Helen Fielding, who would go on to write 'Bridget Jones's Diary', firstly in 'the Independent' newspaper, then as hugely successful novels and big screen hits. She was witty, inventive and great fun to work with. She made a lovely film for the programme about a boy who wanted a big chandelier in his suburban semi. I once told her that on dark nights I would hold a white handkerchief in my hand, so that I would show up when crossing the road. The next day she deposited on my desk a pair of lime-green, knitted fingerless gloves. "They should do the trick,", she advised.

I was disappointed to read a couple of weeks ago that, when asked in an interview about Jimmy Savile's behaviour, she replied that she "assumed everyone knew". Knew what, Helen? That he was a serial rapist? Oh dear, Helen. Not you too!

Ace jingle writer, David Mindel, wrote the theme tune that I chose for the programme. It was a vocal, for which I wrote the lyrics. The pictures for the opening titles changed for each series, and the lyrics had to match the pictures. For example: "If you want to play in a Mexican band, ride a horse in the sea or go sailing on land, if you want to know your value in gold, or be famous when your ten years old," etc. I had to write new words for each series. My lyrics would earn me about eight pounds a show, courtesy of the Performing Rights Society for each transmitted programme. However, if an advertising agency wanted to use a piece of published music, the fee payable was negotiable. David Mindel's melody became very popular and was once voted top 'feel good' theme in an advertising magazine, hard to believe after the events of 2012. As the lyric writer, I would receive a percentage of the fee, even if only the melody was used. David always meticulously sent me my share. It was used as background music for several TV commercials, including one for the Co-op. Their animated commercial featured several line-drawn sheep. It must have been done in such a way that it did not imply that Co-op customers were like sheep. The 'baa baa baa' of the chorus became a bleat for these animated lambs. Thanks to David's negotiations with the agency, the bleats, which I could claim to have 'written', provided me with a cheque for four thousand pounds.

At the height of the media hysteria about Savile one journalist suggested that the BBC 'had egg on its face', when it was discovered that the man who wrote the British entry for the 2013 Eurovision Song Contest, David Mindel, had also written the 'Jim'll Fix It' theme music. A disgrace! I suggested that the people who manufactured Savile's tracksuits should also be hounded down immediately.

At about the same time as my first association with Savile, I was getting fed up with my nomadic existence. I was more or less of no fixed abode and could put all my possessions into one suitcase. There was a string of girlfriends, in whose flats or houses I frequently stayed, whilst always renting a modest flat for myself somewhere. There was Hilary Pritchard, a wonderful bubbly woman, who was then appearing on 'Braden's Week' as a British answer to Goldie Hawn on 'Rowan and Martin's 'Laugh-In'. One of her co-presenters was Esther Rantzen. We did not use the word 'stalker' in those days, but Hilary had one called Mark. We discovered him one night at the top of a ladder outside Hilary's bedroom window. My reaction was to try to push him and the ladder down into the garden. Thank heavens I failed.

After Hilary came Gillian Hawser, a more serious actress, who was at Trinity with me, although we did not know each other well there. Her father, Lewis Hawser, was a brilliant Q.C. The family lived in Eaton Place, Belgravia. It was all quite posh and interesting people came to dinner there. Leo Abse, the M.P. was a guest one evening. He was a fascinating talker. He was famed for having introduced more Private Members' Bills than any other parliamentarian in the twentieth century, the most significant of which were his campaigns to reform the laws regarding divorce and the decriminalisation of male homosexuality.

Sponsoring Leo Abse's bill in the House of Lords was Lord Arran, also a passionate supporter of animals' rights, who attempted to establish a bill outlawing the hunting of badgers. The bill decriminalising homosexuality succeeded, but the bill outlawing badger-hunting did not receive enough support. Asked why one had failed and the other succeeded, Lord Arran replied that there were not many badgers in the House of Lords.

Gillian's father bought her a house near Brook Green, Shepherd's Bush and I moved in, a terrible mistake and we were ill-suited. Not long after we parted, she married someone far more suitable. Some years later she must have had an affair with one-time BBC Head of Music and Arts, Humphrey Burton, because they have a child, the totally brilliant Clemency Burton-Hill, who after gaining a double first at Cambridge, went on to fame as the presenter of 'The Last Night of the Proms' and 'Young Musician of the Year'.

The thing I learned from my time living with Gillian was how nice it would be to have a house of my own. With £600 in the bank, I was not sure if that was going to be possible. I wanted to be near work and chose Acton, a fairly grim inner suburb a couple of miles west of Shepherd's Bush. My annual salary was about £2,500 and the house I wanted cost £11,000. By taking an 'endowment' mortgage, that is one linked to an unencumbered life assurance policy, and borrowing some of the deposit from the bank, I was just able to be acceptable to the Nationwide Building Society. I had virtually no furniture and it was a bit of a struggle to start with. Various BBC bachelors became lodgers over the next years to help pay the mortgage for the house in the oddly-named Dordrecht Road, Acton.

If someone today had an equivalent job to mine then, but no capital, the mortgage required would be at least a million pounds, which would be much more than ten times the purchaser's salary. Out of the question. What has happened? A two-class society seems to have sprung up, where the only ways a typical wage-earner can 'get on the property ladder' is by either borrowing from parents or becoming a drug-dealer.

Bruce Milliard was at one time my lodger. One evening he and I were at a record company's reception in the centre of London. They were promoting a new recording artist. The conversation went something like this:

ME: "Let's get out of here, Shall we go to a pub?"

BRUCE: "Yes. Which pub shall we go to? Which is your favourite?"

ME: "My favourite pub is the Engine Inn near St. Ives, Cornwall."

BRUCE: "Well, let's go there, then."

So we did. We had no luggage, no change of clothes or anything, but we took a taxi to Paddington and were just in time to get tickets for the sleeper. We got on board the train and spoke to the sleeping car attendant. "Just wait until the train moves off, if you don't mind, lads" he said. Puzzled, we waited as advised. As soon as the train started to creak away from the station, we showed our tickets to the attendant.

"Oh. You've got tickets!" he said in surprise, "Sorry to have kept you waiting" and showed us to our berths. He must have had a nice little racket going, since the sleeping car attendant is also the ticket collector. I wonder how often he was able to cater for 'standby passengers' in that way.?

The following morning, as we got off the train at six a.m. in deserted St Erth station, the previous evening's jolly wheeze did not seem such a good idea, especially since there were no taxis and it was starting to drizzle. We took the little connecting train into St Ives, found somewhere to have breakfast and waited for Woolworths to open, so that we could buy some form of rainwear for Bruce. I think I had a Parka to keep me dry. Bruce was a big lad and all that Woolworth's could come up with was a ladies' plastic mac but it was better than nothing. Luckily the following day was a non-working Saturday. 'The Engine' would not open until ten thirty and we were leaning on the door there at opening time. I explained to Jack House, the flamboyant landlord, that I had brought my friend to the Engine Inn, because it was the best pub in England. Jack said:

"Well, you just lost your bet, because this pub isn't in England; it's in Cornwall!"

But it was time to 'grow up'. I was in need of some domesticity. A year later I was married to Auriol, a sweet-natured researcher at the BBC. All went well for a while, but we were not really suited. She wanted children; I did not, or so I thought at the time. She drifted into an affair, which was probably as much my fault as hers and after four years together we divorced. Auriol's father had been managing director of Tyne-Tees Television, before being ousted in a business coup. He still had some of the trappings of a boardroom man, including a Coutt's Bank account. Because of him I acquired an account of my own at Coutt's and used to enjoy visiting their branch in the Strand, where 'my' manager wore a frock coat for work. I have heard it said that to have an account at Coutt's, you must have at least a million pounds in the bank. If only!

I gave up my Coutt's account only five years ago and came down with a bump. Gone was my flashy chequebook. Now I am with the down-to-earth Nationwide Building Society. *Sic transit Gloria mundi.*

Helen Fielding's boyfriend, when she was with the programme, was John Lloyd, an outstanding producer and the principal brain behind 'Not the Nine o'clock News' and 'Blackadder'. I think he must have put in a good word for me with Stephen Fry and Hugh Laurie, because I was appointed to produce and direct their forthcoming sketch show, 'A Bit of Fry and Laurie'. I had a very jolly first meeting with the two of them in Douglas Adams's*(Footnote:

Author of 'The Hitchhiker's Guide to the Galaxy') house in Islington, which he had lent Stephen briefly during his absence in the USA.

Stephen was very keen on I.T. and they wrote their scripts using the first Apple computer I had seen. They had me record my voice saying things like, "Get on with it!", and 'Don't just sit there!" which would play automatically at random intervals to try to prevent them doing everything else except writing the script

The first transmission, a Christmas 'try out', was well received. I was delighted to be congratulated by Ben Elton, whom I admire enormously. The first series was very funny and clever but it was to some extent a specialist programme and did not get the huge viewing figures that Stephen and Hugh were hoping for. It is at times like this that the producer tends to become the scapegoat. I think Hugh had been enjoying the cut and thrust of 'Blackadder' rehearsals, where I imagine scriptwriter and cast could argue about each line of the script. I think there was cut, but perhaps not enough thrust for him. He wanted confrontation. Hugh once asked me, "Why do you always agree with me?" For the second series a script editor and a second producer, both Cambridge Footlights contemporaries, were brought in. If confrontation was sought, they had chosen the wrong people. I have never heard such sycophancy. The atmosphere was good however, and it was useful to have the associate producer on the studio floor, while I was in the gallery, directing the cameras. Hugh could never get used to the studio audience and would hate them intensely, while waiting for the recording to start. He would sit in his dressing room making V-signs at them through the dressing room wall. Somebody said of him, "Hugh wanted to be a chartered accountant but his parents forced him to go on the stage." I wonder if his huge success, playing Americans with weird accents in the USA, has changed his attitude but I suppose he does not have to encounter his audience there.

Working with Stephen Fry was always a pleasure, although I had no idea he was snorting cocaine constantly at the time, as he revealed later in his memoirs. Some of his expressions from the 'Fry and Laurie' scripts have stayed with us. We still occasionally offer each other 'a cup of nice tea' or state that the weather is 'not too hot but not too mild neither'. I worked on three series and was pleased to get a very friendly autograph on the flyleaf of the published edition of the F&L scripts:

"To R.O., the onlie begetter of the ensuing sketches. With love, adoration and a tiny hint of splendour. Stephen Fry." It could not have been written by anyone else, really!

Being involved with a different type of programme put me in a different market-place. I had a phone call asking me if I would be available to direct 'Spitting Image'. That would have been fun but it was an ITV programme and I was contracted to the BBC.

30.

POLITICS

Most politicians are anti-BBC, because they always think the Corporation favours 'the other side'. The Left thinks there is a Right bias; the Right thinks there is a Left bias. In a way, that should mean the Corporation is maintaining a balance. Margaret Thatcher was more virulent than most in her anti-BBC stance. Her attitude seemed to be that we were a bunch of degenerate pinkoes and possibly homosexual as well. The BBC needed to be punished. She appointed Marmaduke Hussey as chairman, hoping he would tidy the place up and do to the BBC what he had done to Times Newspapers, thus making it more efficient. His Director General, Michael Checkland, was not as compliant as was hoped and was eventually replaced by the inept John Birt. If Thatcher's idea had been to make the BBC more cost-effective and to make cuts in staff levels, she had chosen the wrong man. The expansion in layers of management was exponential. We had to play at competition by trying to estimate the total costs of everything and had to bid for camera crews and studios, as if we were independent production companies, which was pure fairyland, because the infrastructure was there and more or less immutable. There was for example a lawn at Ealing Film Studios, then part of the BBC. It was very useful for 'pick up shots' and 'cutaways' needed to smooth out an edit. You could return from a shoot with a crew and take a couple of extra shots on this bit of grass. But then came 'total costing'. Everything had to be bid for and paid for, including this lawn. No producer was going to eat into the programme budget by paying extra for the use of this tiny bit of land. Therefore nobody used it. The annual cost of owning this bit of grass was estimated at several thousand pounds. Therefore, if anyone had wanted to apply to include filming on the lawn, he or she would have been the only person in that year to use it and the estimated annual cost would go entirely on their programme's budget. Instead we would take extra shots, if necessary, in a park round the corner for no charge. The lawn remained empty and unused. That's how realistic 'total costing' was.

As the years at the Corporation progressed, so did the size of the bureaucracy. The arrival of John Birt as Director General in 1992 saw a massive surge in the number of managers at the same time as stringent cuts in the size of programme budgets. Early on in the Birt years I went to one of the many seminars he favoured, usually with incomprehensible titles such as 'Dealing with Change' or 'Maintaining Connectivity'. As spokesperson for my group I was able to ask the visiting Managing Director a question I had been longing to know the answer to: "Year after year we are told to reduce our programme budgets. Is Management setting us a good example, therefore, when it constantly seems to grow in number?"

I went on to quote the increase in the number of 'Managing Directors' from three to nine. My own department, Television Light Entertainment, used to contain two 'Head ofs'. There were now suddenly nine people with that title. The reason for these phenomena was given by the visiting M.D. In the good old days, he explained, the Corporation simply threw money at problems, but nowadays cash was so tight, that larger management was necessary to control the limited funds. I was able to challenge this assertion and sent a letter to the BBC house magazine, 'Ariel', which, to my surprise, they published. In it I listed the BBC's income from 1965 to 1995, adjusted to the Retail Price Index for the year in question. The figures actually showed that the BBC's real income only decreased in real terms during one period, which was the 'Good Old Days', between 1970 and 1975. In other periods its real income grew. I asked where all the BBC's additional income was going and wondered if it could be to pay the 450% increase in management brought in 'to save money'. There was a reply to my letter from the head of something or other, in which he opined that perhaps the BBC had been 'undermanaged' in the past. Maybe he was right. Instead of making 'The Forsyte Saga' and 'Life on Earth', the BBC could have imported a few more managing directors.

A writer describing the agony of trying to get a decision out of the BBC today, said that the period of waiting was like an 'eternal amber light'. The eternal amber light nowadays does occasionally turn green, when Commissioning Editors finally decide what programmes are going to be made. Senior to the commissioning editors are the Channel Controllers, who employ a 'scheduler' to decide the programmes' transmission times. So the commissioning editors decide what programmes are to be made and the schedulers decide when they are to be transmitted. What there is left for the Channel Controllers to do, I cannot begin to imagine. Recline on couches, drinking nectar, while being fanned by underlings, perhaps. Cuts in management size could so easily pay for over 75s licence fees.

The exact functions of those at the very top of the B.B.C. hierarchical tree have always puzzled me. Many years before the above, the BBC magazine, 'Ariel' published a limerick of mine about Huw Wheldon, famous as a brilliant broadcaster and a wonderful orator. At that time he held the title of 'Managing Director, Television'.

> I have always been puzzled by Huw,
> His critics are scattered and fuw,
> I know everyone claps,
> When he talks to the chaps,
> But what does he actually duw?

Titles at the B.B.C. got grander and grander as the years went by. When I arrived, the man in charge of radio was called, 'Director, Radio' and the man in charge of television, 'Director, Television'. Later on, these Directors were called 'Managing Directors'. I always thought that there could be only one managing director but with the arrival of John Birt as Director General, managing directors started popping up all over the place. I think eventually there were nine of them. I calculated by extrapolation that by the year 2047 everyone working at the B.B.C. would be a managing director.

I often wondered how I would be as a manager, although I was not the type to be considered to join their ranks. They tended to see themselves as a priesthood, a caste with a mystique of their own. Huw Wheldon once said that there were only two jobs worth having at the BBC. One was Director General, the other, Producer. I think he was right. Being in middle management somewhere would take you away from the very reason for being there – making television. As middle management, you might as well be working for McVities Biscuits. I would have liked to have had a go at management, though. I think I am good at sniffing out bullshit but maybe it is not the job of middle management to announce that the Emperor or the Director General has no clothes.

Barry Took, co-writer of 'Round the Horne' and other radio hits, became a good friend. He and I would devise imaginary BBC job titles and put them on our office doors. One was 'J.P. Salome , Assistant Head of John the Baptist'. Barry and I forbade ourselves from saying the word 'ladies' without adding, "God bless 'em".

Roger:"Where's Sandra?"

Barry: "She's gone to the ladies."

Both: "God bless 'em."

We would compose for each other what we called 'quotations, first draft', such as

'A thing of beauty is quite nice'. ('quite nice' crossed out and replaced by 'a joy for ever')

'All that glisters is rather shiny' ('rather shiny' crossed out and replaced by 'not gold')

'O cuckoo, shall I call thee bird or not?' ('not' crossed out and replaced by 'but a wandering voice?')*

(*Footnote: which reminds me of A.E. Houseman's variation on the quotation, which appeared as a 'Punch' cartoon. First don:"O, Cuckoo, shall I call thee bird, or but a wandering voice?" Second don: "State alternative preferred , with reasons for your choice.")

Barry Took was script editor to the department, thereby being frequently in touch with the 'Monty Python' team. I was a bit miffed to see some of our 'first draft quotations' appear in a Monty Python Annual. Ah, well, they were as much Barry's as mine.

When I look at the BBC news transmissions on television now, I feel sorry for the ant-sized people, just visible in the foreground of the wide-shot, sitting huddled next to each other at their open-plan desks with budget airline spaces between them. I say 'their' desks, but they are not their desks; they are everybody's desks and nobody's desks. It's called 'hot-desking' and it sounds terrible. Where do people put their sandwiches? I bet the big bosses, who no doubt advocate 'hot-desking', have their own single offices with an outer door that shuts and a hospitality cabinet to put their sandwiches in.

Things were so pleasantly different for us in the Television Centre, White City, London in the sixties and seventies. Sometimes the environment felt more like university than a workplace. It is a circular building, which made it difficult for Colin Charman to practise his squash shots against a curved wall in the corridor but that did not stop him. We each had our own desk, where you could keep all your reference material and your sandwiches and feel psychologically secure. The offices had doors into the corridor, which could be closed for private meetings, and to reduce the noise of squash balls against the wall.

The bosses had 'hospitality cabinets'. One of the duties of the B.B.C. waitresses was to keep these drinks cupboards topped up. Ace waitress, Lill, told us a nice little bit of gossip about the Managing Director's hospitality cabinet. "I was topping up the single malts in M.D.'s cupboard this morning," she told us, while serving us in the canteen, "and, blimey, he can't arf lower 'em."

POLITICS

I am not given to writing graffiti but when one of the Otis Elevator Company's lifts broke down, a notice was pinned to the doors, saying, 'Lift out of order'. I could not resist adding neatly at the top of the notice, "Miss Otis regrets".

31.

PERNICKETY

I have always been interested in accents and pronunciations. With old age that has developed into a grumpy old man-ism about the way things are said. In my lifetime the way the language is spoken has changed enormously. When I was a child, an East End Londoner would pronounce 'I'm going home' *'Oim gowing howm'*. Now that sounds more like *'I'm guying hime'*.

Pronunciation letter T is fast disappearing, even at the B.B.C. It requires a lot more physical effort to drop the T in 'water' than to sound it, but fashion is all. I heard the brilliant broadcaster, Amol Rajan, who is also a T-dropper, on Radio Four the other day having a bit of a struggle in his attempts to eliminate all T sounds from his speech. 'Grumpy of Foissac' wrote to him, not expecting an answer:

> Dear Mr Rajan
>
> In modern English pronunciation it has become essential to drop all internal and terminal Ts (as in 'what' and 'later'). I heard you having a bit of a struggle with the word 'entity' on Radio 4 last week. 'En-i-y' is almost impossible to say without sounding at least the first T. May I suggest that the 'entity' be allowed to join 'potato' as an honourable exception, in which the speaker is permitted to sound the first T and still be 'cool'?

He wrote me a lovely reply, saying that my letter was now pinned to his office wall as a reminder of the dedication of Radio Four listeners. How much that was tongue-in-cheek, I am not sure.

Much has been written about the curious fashion of ending statements as if they were questions. "I was going down the road?"

"I don't know, were you?" I want to reply, "Were you going down the road? You were there."

I think it must a kind of shortcut. Consider an expression such as "He was wearing one of those funny hats, know what I mean?" The "know what I mean" is omitted, but the question mark remains: "He was wearing one of those funny hats?"

Even 'received', 'posh' or what used to be 'B.B.C. English' has changed in my lifetime. I remember the posh pronunciation of 'house and grounds' sounding more like 'hice and grinds' but David Cameron doesn't talk like that. His 'house and grounds' sounds more like Wiltshire to me. The cooing 'oo' sound of old posh has disappeared altogether and been replaced by an 'ee' sound. 'Choose' has become 'cheese'; 'moon' has become 'mean'. 'Book 'has become 'bick'. Interestingly 'You' used to rhyme with the French word 'vous'. Now it rhymes with the French word 'tu'. Maybe it's democratisation.

"What are ye deeing this evening?"

"We're guying to the meavies"

The tiny word 'to' used to be barely audible , when I was a lad. Someone might say "I am going t'take the train t'London". Listen to any talking radio today and you will hear that tiny old 'to' occasionally becomes the enormous word TEW:

What would have been:"We are planning t'move our headquarters t'Salford." has become.

"We are planning TEW move our headquarters TEW Salford." Or, even worse

"We are planning TSEW move our headquarters TSEW Salford."

Translate: "Lick at the mean" (Look at the moon.) "I cheese not tew dee so" (I choose not to do so.)

While I'm here, may I have a moan about usage? I'll be brief. The following letter, which I was delighted to have published in the Times' back in 1983, sums up one of my favourite grouses:

Sir, In "To whom it may concern",(May 24th) Philip Howard speaks of the decline of the remaining inflections in English When making a request on behalf of two people, applicants who write to BBC Television's 'Jim'll Fix It' programme far more often than not say, "Can you fix it for my friend and I?"

I do not think this is an indication of the decline of inflections in the language, so much as the misuse of an inflection, which in this case is a genteelism. Teachers in the past may have told their pupils to avoid such statements as, "My friend and me are going to the zoo," and the result has been a belief that a use of 'my friend and me' is always incorrect.

When the first person singular is used without the conjunction, it is correctly inflected. We never get letters saying, "Can you fix it for I?"

Roger Ordish,
Producer, Light Entertainment Department, BBC Television.

Talking of personal pronouns, the words 'you' and 'I' seem to have been permanently replaced by 'yourself' and 'myself'.

"I'll have a word with yourself next week", or "Thanks for all the lovely cards you sent to Lorna and myself."

And how about this one?

Person at desk: "What was your surname?"

I am tempted to reply, and sometimes have: "What WAS my surname? It IS Ordish and always has been."

Oh, and "Have you got a Boot's card at all?"

What do you mean, 'at all'? Do you mean 'have I got a Boot's card to any extent?', 'have I got a bit of a Boot's card?' Maybe I have the top right-hand corner of a Boot's card or I have a Boot's card but only on Wednesday mornings. But it doesn't really matter at all, does it? Not at all, at all.

PERNICKETY

When I was little, if I fell over and cut my knee, people might ask me. "Are you all right?". Now they say it to me, whenever I go into a shop.

And, while I'm whingeing, the word 'and' seems to be disappearing to be replaced by 'plus', certainly in television advertising, anyway.

"Plus you get a free upgrade to Premier Economy!", "Plus kids go free!"

Enough of this, I'm just popping out for some fish plus chips. Then I'll need to nip into Holland plus Barrett for some indigestion tablets.

And 'in future' has become the omnipresent 'going forward'.

Accents in 'Eastenders' can be a challenge, especially in the lines spoken by actor Jake Wood, who plays the character, Max Branning. Here is my phonetic representation of one of his lines: "Swear cum urea."

What was he saying? It was "So, how come you are here?"

Or, try this one:

"Air bairt cinq tweet?". "How about something to eat?"

32.

ODD ONE OUT

Jim Moir, a dear friend and my best man twice, was made head of the sub-department of our group, known as 'Variety', which sounds an old fashioned word now with echoes of music halls, George Robey and Harry Lauder. Jim's new posting meant that someone had to take over the shows he was scheduled to produce. I was the someone else. Jim would have been running a Paul Daniels quiz programme called, 'Odd One Out'. I took his place. A nasty, scrofulous little man, desperate for promotion, who was scheduled to direct the shows, phoned Paul Daniels and the production team, asking them to attend a meeting. He did not tell me, the producer, that he had called the meeting. I suppose his plan was to sideline me, so that he would be the one to be consulted rather than me. His afflicted, flaky skin was probably caused by his devious mental state. Despicable, but some people would kill for promotion! His plot did not work and Paul Daniels, the lovely Debbie McGee and I became great friends for life.

One of the contestants on one of the shows was a woman called Susan Wishlade. When I saw her and heard her in rehearsal, I was bowled over. Love at first sight, I suppose. We discovered that we both lived in Richmond, Surrey, loved laughter and the rest was geography.

Susie was off almost immediately to California with her seven-year-old son, Tim.

We both had time for reflection but after Susie's return, feelings were the same on both sides. We got on so well together and laughed a lot. Perhaps we both have what is now so dreadfully called a 'GSOH' (good sense of humour) but a GSOH is better than NSOH. Perhaps there is another spectrum there, on which we all have our position.

Susie and her son moved in to my house in Albert Road, Richmond and in 1984 we got married in the local Registry Office followed by a blessing from a very showbizzy vicar in the nearby Saint Matthias church. My parents were present and it heartened me to see how my mother approved of Susie. Susie could be forgiven for remembering that my mother said to her. "I can't decide if you look more like Elizabeth Taylor or Joan Collins."

It suddenly occurred to me that I would like to father a child after all. Susie had had miscarriages in the past and we were both getting on in years. She was happy to try. There were more miscarriages. Then Lulu was conceived and she was determined to hang on in there, despite the fact that pregnant Susie accompanied me on a filming trip to the Seychelles, which necessitated her bouncing around on unmade roads in a Mini Moke. The subjects of our filming were a man and his girlfriend, who lived together. He was forever asking his partner to marry him. Every time he asked her, she would reply, "Only if we get married in the Seychelles". So, thanks to the programme, they did.

It all worked very well and Lulu was born three months after the Seychelles trip. In my first marriage I had not wanted children, regarding them as a nuisance. Oh, what a mistake! The arrival of this beautiful little bundle was quite overwhelming. O.K. you dads out there, I know, I know. I'll shut up, but, oh, what magic! I loved holding her and just looking at her. Lulu seemed never to cry at night and Susie breast-fed her so quietly in the dark, that I hardly ever woke. And how delightful three or four years later to be sharing a Great Western Railway cabin with her on her way to visit my parents in Cornwall. Lulu and I would watch out of the cabin window together, as the train weaved its way through the lights of London, until I would finally tuck Lulu into the lower berth, as the city lights dwindled.

The imminent arrival of Lulu meant we needed a bigger house. We sold our little terrace cottage in fashionable Richmond and bought a larger one in not quite so fashionable Twickenham for only five thousand pounds more.(£110.000). That house has since been valued at over two million. The new house was very near the bridge into Richmond, which made the estate agents describe the area as 'Richmond Bridge'.

The most popular local junior school for the middle-class was 'The Old Vicarage'. So popular was it that, in the year of her birth it was already too late for Lulu, born on June 30th, to get a place there. The waiting list was full. The alternative was a convent in Twickenham. I could not bear the thought of Lulu being taught by nuns. However, the dilemma was sorted, when the Old Vicarage was finally able to squeeze her in. The school was only a short walk across Richmond Bridge, although little Lulu was almost next to the CO_2 being pumped out by the endless stream of cars across the bridge. We feared it might make her asthmatic. We enjoyed getting involved with the school, Susie becoming secretary of the Parent-Teacher Association and I compiling quizzes for their fund-raising events. On one occasion I even sang some of the questions. In one round of the quiz the contestants had to give the correct occupations in songs, where I had changed the job description of the subject. Example: what should the profession in this song be: "You'll forget the plastic surgeon who whistled o'er the lea,?" Answer: 'the little ploughboy'. I think the parents at the Old Vicarage were more likely to be plastic surgeons than ploughboys.

Lulu started off afraid of water but went through a transformation after a few years to become a member of the Roedean junior swimming team. Her swimming teacher while she was at primary school said to the class during one lesson: "Now, girls, I want each of you to jump into the water either as an arrow or as a star." When it got to Lulu's turn, the teacher asked, "Louise, are you going to go in like a star or like an arrow?" Lulu replied. "I'm going to go in like a person."

I wanted Lulu to have the best education money could buy and decided on Roedean, against her headmistress's advice. My daughter's school reports had described her as a 'free spirit', which indeed she is. Roedean was not the place for free spirits. On reflection I think Bedales (which we did visit) would have suited her better. She finally came into her own at a wonderful sort of boarding sixth form college in Surrey called Hurtwood House, a place for free spirits, where she made many good friends and was able to express her artistic skill to the utmost. I used the word 'skill' there in the singular. For some reason 'skill' is always used in the plural now. People say 'his darts skills' for example. Surely there is only one skill in darts – making the dart land where you want it to.

33.

SECRETS

Shortly before I left the BBC, I produced what was probably the last of its type, a lavish spectacular, variety programme called, 'Secrets' which was the name of an imaginary night club, created for the show. It was built around the amazing conjuring talents of Paul Daniels and other visiting magicians but featured also dancers and comedians. Paul was a brilliant conjuror, particularly in the execution of 'close-up' magic.

Generally I accepted magic as 'magic' and did not try to find out how things were done, although it is not giving anything away to reveal that, if Debbie McGee had disappeared from a locked trunk, she had either contorted herself into a masked corner of the trunk, or had 'gone south' through a hole in the bottom of the trunk and into a rostrum. However, I was determined to find out the secret of one particular close-up trick, in which Paul would hold a pack of cards in his left hand, showing the cards to the camera and audience. There might be, for instance, the Queen of Hearts showing at the top of the pack in his left hand. Demonstrating that there was nothing in his right hand, Paul would then pass it across the Queen of Hearts. In the two seconds that it took his hand to obscure the queen, it would become, say, the Ace of Spades. He would show once more that there was still nothing in his right hand. We had this trick in close up on the recording tape, which takes twenty-five pictures every second. I slowed the tape down, so that I could examine it frame by frame and was none the wiser. The Queen had turned into the ace. That's magic. No, that's skill. Paul Daniels practised as carefully and as frequently as a virtuoso violinist would.

Part of my job as producer of 'Secrets' was to select cabaret acts with a magic theme. The job once took me to Paris to see a brilliant double act, all in mime, by a couple who called themselves Vik and Fabrini. One played a mad scientist, the other a sort of Frankenstein's monster. It was very funny. Nice work, if you can get it, being paid to sit with a glass of champagne and watch the dancing girls and the acts at the Crazy Horse Saloon in Paris. I did not book the 'speciality' magic acts, which was left to Paul's entourage of Magic Circle members. Some of these performers seemed to belong to another age. Whenever I take a sharp knife out of a kitchen drawer now, I still think of Hans Moretti, whose act included throwing deadly-looking blades while blindfolded, narrowly missing his trusting wife, as the knives formed a neat semicircle around her.

My Eurostar train back from Paris was delayed sufficiently for the passengers to be compensated with one standard class return trip to Paris each. I suggested to the man in the seat next to me that we tossed a coin, so that, whoever won, would have two return tickets. He won. He was interested to hear about the 'Secrets' programme and I invited him to come to one of the recordings, which he did. He turned out to be Sir Alan Budd, one of Margaret Thatcher's top economic advisers.

34.

WORDS, WORDS. WORDS

Travelling by tube into work from Richmond to Shepherd's Bush, I would find myself making anagrams in my head of station names or words in advertisements. Wondering if I might have a particular skill in that useless activity, I joined Richmond Scrabble Club, who met every Wednesday evening. I soon realised that what had been designed as a simple family board game could become an obsession. If you want to succeed in scrabble, you have to learn a lot of obscure words. The more words you know, the better you will be at the game but that way a kind of madness can lie, as King Lear would have said, although he was not talking about scrabble. I settled for knowing at least all the two-letter words and most of the threes. There are over a hundred two letter words, including 'AA', a volcanic rock, 'XI' a Greek letter and 'QI', vital energy. I then tried to learn all 1,347 permitted three-letter words. I never quite achieved that goal but progressed to trying to memorise all the four-letter words that can be made by adding one letter to one of the acceptable three letter words. Canny players can also study 'The Book of Scrabble Lists', which will show the statistically most likely six letter combinations to appear on your 'rack' and what seven letter words can be made with the addition of one more tile. For example, 'RETAIN' is a frequent combination. By adding B to that combination you can make 'ATEBRIN', an anti-malaria drug. By adding the letter G you can make 'TEARING', 'INGRATE', 'GRANITE' and others. I tried to learn what seven letter words can be made from the fifty most frequently occurring six letter combinations. If you think that's insane, let me tell you about Nigel Richards from New Zealand. Nigel has been world English language scrabble champion four times. Where could he go from there? Although he does not speak the language, Nigel studied the French scrabble dictionary for two months and went on to win the French scrabble championship in 2015 and 2018 without knowing the meanings of the words he was laying down.

In our scrabble club in Richmond, Surrey, there was a comparable man called Nick, who was a lavatory attendant in Kingston. He was a sort of 'Rain Man' or 'idiot savant' and, when not too involved in his work, would study and learn by heart large numbers of words from the Scrabble dictionary. His conversational vocabulary was limited, however, for he generally did not know the meanings of the words he played. I can remember sometimes playing a not very obscure word against him, something like 'overlap' perhaps. Nick might say, "Ooh I haven't heard of that one. Must remember it."

Occasionally during the library hush of play in the club, Nick would cry out, "Ah, well, it's only a game!" When I am losing badly, I remember Nick's cry. It is only a game. Or is it?

Nowadays it is possible to play computer scrabble on-line against real people. It is a terrible time-waster. An interesting aspect of it is that a lot of players cheat, or it certainly seems as if they do. I often play an unknown person, whose scrabble vocabulary seems limited to average. There is a long pause before the next move, while presumably the other player is consulting an online anagram app. A obscure seven letter word that I have never heard of then appears and my opponent wins. I do not absolutely know that they are cheating, but it seems very likely. It does not really matter but what a strange kind of victory that must be.

It sounds impressive when I say that I have come second three times in the Mensa Scrabble championship, but I have to admit that the best scrabble players in Mensa probably do not go in for that competition. One of the players I lost to in the final was Joyce Cansfield, who had been UK national scrabble champion and compiled crosswords for 'the Times' and 'Listener'. I do have a teapot to show that I won one round of the television game show, 'Countdown', but Joyce was the champion of the first-ever 'Countdown' series.

Apart from the Scrabble I have not been involved in any other Mensa activities for some time. Back in 1996 I was the compère of a rather splendid stage show at Wyndham's Theatre, London for a one night stand. It was the Mensa Variety Show. Several Mensa members did their highly talented turns, mostly musical, which I linked with my own script from that famous stage. I recounted various theatrical anecdotes, including my favourite story about the actress, Coral Browne. The story does not work without a swear-word in the punch line. My ten-year old daughter was at the show, sitting in a box with my wife. I apologised in advance to my daughter. I thought my wife could cope. This is the tale: Coral Browne had just become a convert to Roman Catholicism and was extremely enthusiastic, as only converts can be. As she was just leaving the Brompton Oratory after mass one morning, two camp theatrical dressers, who knew her well, spotted her as she walked reverentially towards them along Knightsbridge.

"Hallo, Coral, Babe!", they cooed, "Are you alright, darling?". Coral Browne eyed them coldly and muttered through gritted teeth, "Fuck off. I'm in a state of grace!"

35.

LEWES

In 1997 we sold the Richmond house (should have kept it and let it, of course). We chose Lewes for our new home, since it is an interesting town and was near to Brighton, where Roedean is.

In Richmond I would sometimes travel in to work with a friend from our road, who worked in the 'city'. He hated his job and could not wait for it to finish. On good days I could not wait to get to work. It saddens me when I hear comparatively young people looking forward to or choosing early retirement. Since I had had an interesting job, the last thing I wanted to do was retire. When I left the BBC after thirty-three years continual service, I tried for a while to find freelance work in television. I was not successful. Then I tried proposing television formats. There seems to be a Catch-22 about trying to suggest programme ideas. The all-powerful commissioning editors deal only with major production companies. I had a registered production company but it was only a one-man band. Commissioning editors will not even look at programme ideas sent in by unknown production companies. An individual with a programme idea has to submit it to one of the big, established companies, companies who can take commissioning editors out to lunch. The principal production companies do not want formats from outside. They want in-house ideas, from which all profits accrue to them with no royalties to be paid to a third party. (see 'head', and 'brick wall'). I had a few programme ideas, for which I made passable low-budget demonstration videos. Showing these to non-flattering, professional colleagues, I got favourable comments as to their viability for television but it was a pointless exercise. You cannot beat a cartel. I decided instead to downgrade my ambitions and with part of my retirement settlement bought one of the latest professional video cameras and a state-of-the-art video editing programme in its own computer. Not being a naturally technical person, I also paid for a course of instruction from the brilliant company in Brighton, who had put together my computer with all its editing add-ons. The kit produced pictures, which - if not the very best - were of sufficiently high quality to be acceptable for broadcasting. I founded 'Heavenly Productions' as a limited company and, operating from our newly bought house in Lewes, Sussex, advertised myself as: 'ex-BBC television director provides broadcast-quality video at remarkably low prices'. I created a website and joined a local business networking group, who met for breakfast every Monday at 7.30 a.m. Odd jobs started to trickle in and eventually the company was earning me an extra twenty thousand a year to add to my reasonably comfortable BBC pension. I was in the luxurious position of being an entrepreneur, which I enjoyed enormously, without having to keep the wolf from the door. I made several training videos for a highly successful security firm, Sabrewatch, whose clients included Selfridges and Marks and Spencer, and secured a regular job updating the videos showing in the visitor centre in a wonderful park called Wakehurst Place in Sussex, which belongs to Kew Gardens and is their country arm. I even made a television commercial with the disappointingly low budget of one thousand pounds

I soon learned that, if I wanted to increase my turnover, I should also offer myself as a wedding videographer. I advertised in wedding magazines and websites. Eventually I landed quite a few wedding bookings. 'Have your wedding videoed by ex-BBC Television director'. My former work colleagues considered it rather infra-dig, that I should take on so lowly a task but in truth it required more skill than anything I had done to date. In that job you are a news reporter and the cameraman, everything is going to happen only once, but you must not get in anybody's way. You need to be in the middle of everything, while at the same time trying to be invisible .It was hard work but rewarding, if you got it right. The most rewarding part was the computer editing, with which I was familiar at the BBC, although there it was a matter of getting a professional editor to do the job for me, rather than doing it myself. Chris Booth, a good friend, edited nearly all the 'Fix it' programmes and I learned a lot from his technique, when I had to try to do it alone. With a high-definition camera every frame you shoot (at twenty five frames a second) is of sufficiently high quality to become a photograph in the wedding album, but for some reason the traditional wedding photographer was always considered first in the pecking order. Most big weddings would go without the video man, rather than sacrifice the photographer. As a sort of news cameraman, you needed to be ready for the next event before it happened and no-one ever seemed to know what would be happening next - not even the Best Man. And you cannot walk up to the priest and ask him to do a re-take.

"Sorry, bishop, but could we do that bit again? Camera wasn't ready."

There were some memorable moments: a groom so overcome with emotion, that he could not manage the words of the vows, despite the alarmed looks from the bride, trying to calm him through his sobs. There was a vicar, who fluffed one of the prayers, turned to the camera and said, "You'll be able to edit that out." I, of course, left it in. One customer called to ask if I covered funerals. He had recently lost his young wife tragically through cancer. The funeral was a splendid affair with a procession through Billingshurst in Sussex led by the widower in a veiled topper, ahead of four black horses, adorned with plumes of matching feathers and drawing a glass-sided hearse. A couple of years later the same man rang me and asked if I remembered him. Of course I did, I assured him "Well, I'm getting married in June," he said , "and you did such a lovely job on Julie's funeral, that we'd like you to film our wedding." So I did.

The dreariest part of the wedding videographer's job is the speeches. The father of the bride can often be the worst, particularly if he is a put-upon man. He sees his speech as an opportunity to have his say without interruption, maybe for the first time in his life. My record for the longest father-of-the bride speech was forty-two minutes. My tape ran out during his oration and I had hurriedly to replace it but, if anyone was still awake watching the final cut, I don't think they would have noticed the gap, as he droned on and on. I recommended in my notes to potential customers, "Even if you are Stephen Fry, don't speak for more than six minutes" but people seemed to think that making a long speech was somehow funny and would boast about the length of the forthcoming oration in their opening words . The camera saw it otherwise with children squabbling on the floor and adults creeping out of the room 'for a cigarette' and not coming back in.

There was a brilliantly funny American rabbi, a bit like Jackie Mason, who officiated at a lavish Jewish wedding I filmed. "And now we come to the vows," he announced to the happy couple, "Affirmative answers would be preferred."

At another expensive affair in the Brighton Grand Hotel (of Mrs. Thatcher fame) the Best Man said rather indelicately in his speech, "I'll keep my speech short, because I know Ryan can't wait to get Sharon's knickers off..." The Best Man was interrupted by a cry from the bride just along the table from him, "I ain't got none on!" Such lovely people.

I filmed an expensive wedding at Highclere Castle near Newbury in Hampshire. The castle is better known now to viewers as 'Downton Abbey' in the very successful television series, home of Lord Grantham. It is a beautiful setting for a wedding but not at its best without Maggie Smith's one-liners.

The grandest wedding I shot took place in what was described as "Scotland's finest hotel", the Inverlochy Castle in Fort William. I have just Googled the hotel "£650 for one room for one night" says the advertisement. Jane, the bride-to-be. contacted me and we met for coffee in Selfridges. She was planning to get married that June, she explained. She and her fiancé both worked for Smith, Kline,

Beecham, where he was the head of finance. They had booked the entire hotel for three days of celebration and she wanted me to cover the whole event. I said that I would love to do the job, but added that my wife Susie would have to come as my assistant and that we would require a sleeping car on the train in both directions and a hotel in Fort William for three nights. I said, too honestly perhaps, that I was sure she could find somebody in Glasgow to do the job but she said, no, she wanted me to do it. I did not meet the groom, who was working in the U.S.A. at the time. We made all our arrangements and I sent her an estimate of the cost. She did not blink.

A few days before the great event, the bride-to-be called me to say that a disaster had occurred. Alan had suffered a heart attack and was in intensive care in a New York hospital. "However," she said, "he is determined to go ahead with the wedding and on his first class flight to Scotland he will be accompanied all the way by his heart surgeon."

When I met Alan on day one of the events, he looked more suited to a funeral than a wedding. He was as grey as concrete. But he made it through the three days, which included golf, shooting, riding, a lavish meal each evening with an ever open bar tab and there was something else, oh, yes, the marriage ceremony. It was mid June and we were in northern Scotland. A bit of daylight was still evident at 11.30 pm. I think 'gloaming' is the word in that part of the world. Not really the time for fireworks but they were let off anyway. I do not know at what time the last stragglers went to bed but at seven o'clock the next morning Alan had arranged for a lone piper to parade along each corridor of the hotel.

A few weeks later the new bride came to visit me for a preview of the wedding video. She saw Susie's bronze sculpture of my head and was very impressed by it. "Could you do one of Alan?" she asked. Just the casting of a bronze head costs nearly four thousand pounds, but that was not a problem.

"But, if I have one of him, I suppose he'll want one of me," she added.

So, Susie got a commission to do the two real bronze portrait heads. In the end her bill for the sculptures was bigger than my bill for the video. Jane and Alan had been living together for fifteen years before that magnificent Scottish wedding but for some reason we kept in touch with them and discovered that, after less than two years, Alan had started an affair with someone and Jane had chucked him out.

"What happened to his bronze head?" I asked.

"I use it as a doorstop," replied Jane.

I greatly enjoyed making a video for display at Arundel Castle, home of the Dukes of Norfolk. With the hereditary role of Earl Marshal, the Dukes of Norfolk were in charge of great royal ceremonies, such as weddings and funerals. This meant that in the archives at Arundel Castle were miles of cine film footage of those events. I was asked to transfer to video the most interesting items in the collection and then edit them into a sequence for a continuous rolling display to visitors with a commentary that I wrote (with direction) and voiced myself.

Secretary to the Duke was a man called Robert Bruce. Someone asked me: "not Robert THE Bruce?" "No, " I replied, "just Robert A Bruce, I'm afraid."

I made videos for a nearby animal rescue centre, Raystede, which had a television screen showing visitors the centre's latest news. In charge of Raystede was another ex-BBC man, who had rather a brusque manner. He told me that one of his jobs at the BBC had been to answer the telephone to viewers who were responding to the screen message, "If you have been affected by this programme, please call our helpline on 0800 etc."

I could not imagine anyone less suited to being sympathetic with a disturbed caller and we used to imagine how the dialogue might have gone:

"It's only a play, you stupid woman! Those were actors. He's not really dead. That wasn't blood; it was tomato ketchup!"

36.

OPERATICS

In my first term at Tonbridge School our eccentric form master, Philip Bathurst, taught us about Gilbert and Sullivan. He always took a leading role in the school's annual G&S concert. I learned a lot about 'Iolanthe' and acquired a fondness for the Savoy operettas. To my parents' generation Gilbert and Sullivan was old hat but I found Sullivan's music thrilling and Gilberts lyrics clever , if a little heavy-handed at times. I acted professionally very briefly before joining the BBC. Commitments at the Corporation prevented me from performing any more. I was the other side of the camera from then on, except for a three month break, which the BBC allowed me, so that I could appear in a six part revue series for Lew Grade's A.T.V. called 'Broad and Narrow', a Dublin reference, since all the cast were from Trinity College, Dublin. It was a marvellous opportunity but the scripts were pretentious and abysmal. The fact that we had no studio audience was an advantage, since I do not think we would have got many laughs. The A.T.V. thinking was: all you need to do is get some university people and put their revues on television. They had seen 'Beyond the Fringe' and thought anybody could do it. They couldn't. Our director, Albert Locke had moved into television from being what we would now call a stand-up comedian. He said to us something like this: "Look. I don't understand this stuff at all. So just show me where you are going to be and I'll put cameras on it."

A fondness for Gilbert and Sullivan stayed with me and, when I had left the BBC and we had moved to Lewes in Sussex, I was tempted to join the local 'operatic' society. In the eyes of professionals, I was demeaning myself as an amateur. It was as bad as being a wedding videographer but I loved it and from my first audition with Lewes Operatic Society was cast in the very role that

Mr. Bathurst took in the school concert in my first term, the Lord Chancellor in 'Iolanthe'. It was great fun and I was lucky enough to get some other challenging parts including the Major General in 'The Pirates of Penzance' and – best of all – Fagin in 'Oliver'.

GRUMP

I know we old grumpies are renowned for moaning about our phones and computers but, really, sometimes. Things like this: you ask Google how to perform some task on your computer. You are instructed, 'Go to 'Properties'. You search the screen diligently but nowhere does the word 'properties' occur. You can't even start. I have met some I.T. enthusiasts, for whom computers are infallible. "It must be something you are doing incorrectly," I am told. How about this one then, Mr Infallible? Sometimes, not every time, when I try to get on-line, my computer says, "Unable to connect to the proxy server", which for me is total gobbledegook and I have no idea what I should do. What is a 'proxy server' for heavens' sake?

An I.T. consultant, but not a believer in the infallibility of the Internet, has shown me what to do to put it right. It is boring and complicated but it is most definitely not anything caused by me. It just illustrates the randomness of computers.

This evening my i-phone suddenly commanded me "change your date of birth". My I.T. is ordering me to tell a lie. But computers are always right, mere humans always wrong. So I decided to obey. I tried Henry the Eighth's birthday, the twenty-eighth of June 1491 but my phone did not seem to like that. Eager to please, I tried Julius Caesar's birthday, July 13th, 100 BC, but that was not acceptable either. I typed, "You tell me when I was born, then, and I'll agree" but the phone just said, "That is not a date."

Can anyone advise?

Oh, and , if you are having trouble inserting that USB cable, remember USB cables go in the third way round.

37.

FRANCE

In 2007 we sold the house in Lewes and bought a house in the South of France. We should , of course, have let the English house and rented in France. House prices in England continued to rise irrationally, while in France they fell. How can we know these things? Some people seem to.

The French house was a beauty with plenty of space and not too much garden. There was no swimming pool and we had one installed. A giant hole was excavated by a J.C.B. It was pleasing to see a British product being used in France but, of course that was before Brexit. Watching the work, I got the impression that the driver had painted himself into a corner, or dug himself into a corner anyway. I looked at the digger on the wrong side of the hole and asked the driver how he planned to get to the only exit from the garden, which was on other side of the hole.

"Comment allez-vous sortir?"

"Regardez!", he replied and drove the machine straight ahead down into the hole and out the other side.

We had had a swimming pool in Sussex and I had just committed myself to another ten years as pool boy. But there were going to be a lot more hot days in Foissac than there had been in Lewes. I went in as often as I could, if only to bring down the unit cost of a swim.

It is not always actually wrong but English written by a French person is often not what we would actually say. There is a kind of arrogance in not having what you write in a foreign language checked by a native speaker. The Pont du Gard, the famous Roman bridge that once carried an aqueduct across the river Gardon in France illustrates that well. Next to the bridge is a brilliant museum, which must have cost several million euros to put together.

The captions for the exhibits have clearly been translated into English by a French person. For a couple of hundred euros these captions could have been checked by a native English speaker, but no. They were written by some over-confident French person, who wrongly believed their English was perfect. Here is an example:

'Those who enjoy the aesthetic merits of these exhibits may wish to immerse themselves further in the experience.'

It is not exactly incorrect; it is just clumsy and not how we would say it. My sister Jenny, a great Francophile, went to visit one of the châteaux of the Loire and was disappointed to find that it was not open to the public on that day. A notice read:

'Actuellement le château est fermé'. An English translation was added 'Actually the castle is closed'. For a start we would not refer to a Loire château as a 'castle' and 'actuellement' does not mean 'actually'; it means 'now' (or, as the Americans would prefer it 'at this moment in time').

On a tin of 'confit de canard' I saw a list of ingredients in both French and English. In French one of the ingredients was listed as 'matière grasse'. I suppose one would say 'fat content' but the translator called it 'greasy matter'. Appetising!

GRUMP

I object to walking around in clothes that bear a brand name, just so that the manufacturer gets a free advertisement. But maybe an anorak bearing the words 'The North Face' causes the wearer to

hope it will make people think he pops up and down the Eiger most weekends. How subtle this form of advertising is. Other garments, however, with apparently random words on them do not seem to be advertising anything. I once saw a man in a sweater, which announced 'Packhorse 73'. What can it possibly mean? I wonder if the wearer could tell me. More obvious are the England football strips that I see worn in Tesco's on a Saturday morning. I have to say that some of our players look terribly unfit. They are never going to win the World Cup with beer bellies like that.

38.

MEDICINE

In France everything to do with medicine and health is very different from what we are used to in the U.K. The doctors do not get paid as much in France but, from my experience, they seem much more dedicated. My G.P. (généraliste), Dr Ladet, is marvellous but you have to be prepared to wait. I would be told a very specific appointment time, say 09.20, and would find myself still waiting at midday. It was advisable to bring a pair of pyjamas, just in case. He would continue to deal with his patients, until he had done everything he could for them. He told me, and I believe him, that according to the World Health Organisation, France has the best health service in the world. I had two hip replacement operations while I was living in France. In a consultation with the surgeon, he asked me, "When would you like your operation?" Knowing about the year-long queues for operations in the U.K., I could hardly believe my ears."You're asking ME?" After the operation I was offered three weeks in a special recuperation hospital with daily check-ups, excellent meals and physiotherapy twice a day. I don't know how they manage it. Merveilleux!

One important bit of advice from the physiotherapist was that we who were just post- hip operations should not do any movements that involved turning the ankles sharply inwards or outwards too soon. The way she put it was "pas de Charleston!"

Titanium hip joints always set the alarm off in airport security. Before the bell rings, I try to inform the security man that I have these metal plates in my hips. Usually they ignore me and continue in Dalek tones, "Raise your arms", "Turn round", etcetera. I carefully learned how to say it in French, "J'ai deux prothèses de la hanche," but would tend to get the same robotic reaction from the security people. However, on one occasion in the little airport at Nîmes the guard ran his hand-held scanner over my hips and the alarm went off. I said my line about having hip replacements and he put the scanner on his own hip, saying, "Moi aussi!", as the alarm rang for him as well.

The French take their health terribly seriously and will discuss their symptoms endlessly in the chemists. You might see only one person ahead of you in the queue and reckon it will be your turn very soon. Not necessarily. In our local 'pharmacie' there were sometimes three or four pharmacists all dealing with customers at separate counters. But, if one customer had a particularly interesting disorder to describe, the rest of the staff might be summoned to join in the discussion. You could get a hint of how long things were going to take if the customer in front of you had brought a shooting-stick and a packet of sandwiches.

Driving in England is so dull and practical compared with how the French go about it. We tend to drive simply when we want to get from A to B. With the French getting from A to B can be of secondary importance. What really matters is overtaking the car in front of you. Once the car in front has been passed, you can slow down, unless you happen to be in a hurry. I made a Youtube video on the subject, casting myself as a crazed French driving instructor giving advice to foreign motorists. Helpful tips included that the driving mirror was 'only for the ladies, for make-up and so forth' and that the wing-mirrors were there to put your right hand on during hot weather. It got over sixty thousand views – not a huge number by Youtube standards - but more than I had achieved with any of my other Youtube offerings. It also got several 'thumbs down', probably from outraged French drivers, which I have to confess, was rather satisfying.

39.

BREXIT LEFT

We had lived in Richmond for ten years and we lived in Lewes for ten years. After eleven years in France we decided it was time to go back to the U.K. This decision was accelerated by the referendum result, which immediately caused the value of my pension to fall by twenty-five per cent. That shows what the rest of the world thought about Brexit but don't tell the Brexiteers. It makes them so cross. They still think it's wonderful, even if it does mean a fall in the standard of living. Why? I give up.

Selling our house in France was not easy. It was on the market for at least a year, before we found a buyer – even with greedy, lazy French estate agents, who demand five or six percent commission and do very little to earn it. Our potential buyer, we were told was a man who wanted solitude, which our house did not really have. It had a spacious garden but there were other houses nearby. Monsieur Solitude, as we called him did not want a swimming pool. We had one. Nevertheless he wanted our house. The deal was all but signed and sealed, when someone in the village choir asked if anyone knew of a house for sale in Foissac. If we could do a private sale, we would not have to pay the estate agent. The seemingly pleasant enough Dutch couple, who wanted to buy our house, told us that they had an excellent lawyer, who could act for both of us in the sale. We should have smelt a rat immediately. We were being set up. These two Dutch crooks must have been rubbing their hands with glee. It is a complicated story but, in summary, their lawyer, who in fact was working solely for them and not at all for us, told us that 15,000 euros of the sale price would be withheld, until we had left the house on the agreed date, which we did. Had we not left the house, he told us, there would be a fine of 500 euros a day for not leaving, but that did not bother us. We had gone. The sale agreement, which was in French, of course, was very subtly worded. The house should be '*laissée libre*, it said. That we understood to mean 'left free', free of us. It also meant, we were later told, 'free of any of our possessions' I am sure it was deliberately worded in this ambiguous fashion. We asked a good friend in the village to check with Mrs. Van Schidt that everything not wanted had been removed. She said it had, but did not sign anything. This was all part of their scam. Then the lawyer told us he was 'going on holiday'. The holiday he claimed to be on did not, it seems, allow him to read the e-mails we sent asking about the 15,000 euros. After several weeks he wrote saying that we had not removed our furniture from the house, which amazed us. The Dutch crooks had agreed with us weeks before that they would pay us 5,000€ for the furniture, that had been carefully itemised with them. They said that 'for tax reasons' it would be better not to include this agreement in the contract. The lawyer then wrote to say that, yes, we had left the house on time, but had not removed the furniture. The daily 'fine' of 500€ was already being lifted from our funds. The lawyer had waited long enough for us not to be able to do anything about it. By then we were in Yorkshire and the crooks knew full well that we were not in a position to remove the furniture from the house. However, we did manage to ask another wonderful friend to get a charity for the homeless to take the furniture the van Schidts had told us they would be buying. I cannot imagine that the van Schidts have any friends.

The Charity removed the furniture and we received no money but once again Mrs. Van Schidt did not sign anything. They wanted the furniture only as a hostage, so that they could take our 'ransom' money. It was a variation on blackmail. I do not know whether they shared the money with the lawyer but we were totally stitched up. Oh, bring back Monsieur Solitude! If the van Schidts play this trick every time they buy a house, they should be living in a château by now!

In the end the van Schidts got too greedy and tried to tell us that there were still a few things of ours in the garden, sending some blurred photographs of an old table or something and a bill for another 20,000€. Perhaps they were hoping for an additional retirement income of 180,000€ a year, until they had bled us dry. Thanks to a brilliant lawyer in Newcastle, Marcel van Petighen of Anglo-French Law, their further demands were quashed.

When we told our daughter, Lulu, about the scam, she came up with what sounded like the simplest solution to the problem. "Can't you have them killed?", she asked. If only!

40.

RICHMOND, YORKSHIRE

Into my eighties I still get a small amount of paid employment via an agency called 'the Voice Realm'. Like most internet-based enterprises, it makes a lot of money for a very small number of people and very little for anyone else but I am not complaining. We, the voices, send in audition tracks of a script provided on the website. We do not know how many people we are competing with and, on the rare occasions when our voice is chosen, the payment received is modest. You hear of masses of money made by voices in television commercials, a huge payment followed by repeat fees every time the commercial is aired. Advertisers often use well-known performers to voice their commercials, although in only a very few cases do viewers recognise the celeb's expensive voice. It seems a waste of money but then I remember from my brief foray into television advertising, that the more expensive the production, the more the agency receives in its percentage payment. Unfortunately with the Voice Realm it is not like that. The auditions are generally not for television commercials. They are for internal training videos and what they call 'explainer tracks'. Most of the time, I eagerly record my audition and hear nothing more. I do not know how old my voice sounds. Most of the audition pieces state that they require a voice between the ages of thirty and fifty. I should know what to expect, if I am thirty years too old for the job advertised. Occasionally the auditions ask for 'an older sound' and I have sometimes been successful in those auditions. One client was looking for a voice to be used in a theme park, in which the trees spoke to the visitors. I got the job to be a two hundred year old talking beech tree. I can play two hundred. In my last successful audition I had to provide the voice for a penguin, a polar bear and some plankton. It was to do with the polar research ship, 'Sir David Attenborough', the ship which narrowly escaped being called, 'Boaty McBoatface'.

GRUMP: BBC SOUNDS

Oh dear, the poor old Auntie BBC, who provides me with a more than an adequate pension. She gets into a terrible mess sometimes – especially when she is trying to be trendy. BBC Radio has suddenly decided that radio is no longer to be called 'radio' ,but is now 'sounds'. How many senior committee meetings did it take for that momentous decision to be reached, I wonder? Come to think of it, in the early days of television, we used to call it 'sound radio'.

Between you and me, I always knew that what radio produced was sound but I did not give it a trendy label and I did not create a website that made it impossible for anyone without a degree in computer technology to listen to the wireless any more. But that's progress. BBC Sounds invites me to sign in to their website. When I have finally found a password that satisfies what would have defeated Alan Turing, they tell me that all I have to do is sign in and I will stay signed in to their website. Yes, I have found that, when I sign in, I can stay signed in but only for about five minutes. After that I am told that 'all I need to do is sign in, after which I will stay signed in'. You said that last time! It's a mulberry bush situation.

Having somehow managed to listen to the radio yesterday. (Did I say 'radio'? I meant, of course, 'sounds') I heard a self-important American film director telling us that he was 'humbled' by his success. Dare I suggest that he might have been even more humbled, if he had been a failure? This word 'humbled' has now become a means of boasting while pretending not to. We are supposed to be 'humbled' by winning a race. Was Julius Caesar humbled by his successful invasion of Britain? By the way, I am still awaiting an apology from the president of Italy for that incursion.

41.

AND FINALLY

In this book I have been moaning about the BBC, but I love it for what it does and feel horrified now that a wild eyed, unelected 'adviser' (Rasputin, more like) is telling the Prime Minister to get rid of it. Instead of paying the BBC's £154 annual licence, it looks as if viewers will be expected to pay up to £708 a year for a Sky package. Rupert Murdoch must be delighted.

Anyway here we are in what has been voted 'the second best place to live in the United Kingdom', Richmond, North Yorkshire (voted first was Orkney. I think I'll stay in Richmond). We have wonderful neighbours in a lively village, which includes Yorkshire's 'pub of the year'. Next to the pub is the village shop, which is run by volunteers, of whom I am one. I sing in a large local choir. During our Christmas concert , I was looking at some of the tenors and basses in the row in front. Nearly all had white hair or very little hair and many of the ears were adorned with hearing aids but we make a good sound. We have a lovely house. I walked along the road the mile and a half to the nearest bit of moorland and back the other day and only one vehicle passed me. It seems very peaceful and quiet but then I am deaf. My friends and family gave me an unforgettable eightieth birthday party. A quartet of us sang barbershop songs and I wrote a personal limerick for each of the guests. Please indulge me, when I quote two of them:

> Margaret Andrew is ever so posh,
> And also makes exquisite nosh,
> When somebody said,
> "The poor have no bread.",
> She replied, "Let me make them brioches"

> Said our brilliant accompanist, Joan,
> "I do like to set the right tone,
> I'm invited to tea,
> With our local M.P.,
> Should I ask for a scon or a skohn?"

We have just had an election, in which the country had to choose between a compulsive liar and a Marxist. I would suggest the liar was the lesser of two evils, since we might be able to get rid of the liar at the next election. If you look around the world at Marxist nations, it becomes evident that Marxists are not keen on elections that do not keep them in power. Johnson says, "Let's get Brexit done." I think he means, "Let's get Brexit started". It will take years and years of trying to re-negotiate every little detail in the process of leaving the world's third most powerful trading bloc. Ah well. At least Rees-Mogg will have made lots of money, betting on the outcome. So he'll be happy. Unlike poor Prince Harry, for whom my heart bleeds. His sad parting speech to the public included Americanisms such as 'gotten' and was therefore almost certainly dictated by his wife. In his own words I do not think he would have said, "..the decision I have made for my wife and I.." "For my wife and ME," Harry, surely! You are supposed to have had a good education. Driven out by the cruel paparazzi, it seems the couple now have no choice, but to go and do exactly what they want to do. And with only $30,000,000 to live on.

Years ago Clive James fronted a brilliant programme, 'Clive James on Television' in which bizarre clips from various foreign television stations were shown. One clip that was particularly memorable came from Kenya and included a very funny sequence, in which an African actor 'whited up' and did a mickey-taking sketch, imitating a British Colonial Officer. It was very funny. In present-day retrospect I find myself thinking, was it racist in the same way as the much-derided 'Black and White Minstrel Show' was? I did not feel offended by it. Should I have been? But then, I think it was Diane Abbott, who has told us that it was not possible for 'a person of colour' to be racist. Anyway, I don't have to worry about that, thank Goodness.

The saddest thing is hearing that some individuals at universities have taken it upon themselves to ban from participating in Union debates anyone, with whose ideas they disagree. The favourite hate-word these self-appointed arbiters use is 'fascist', which is hurled at anyone who is not 'woke' enough to conform with their particular set of rules. To my mind their attitude is only one step away from burning books, which do not toe the party line. Who was it, who used to burn books, now? I think it was the Fascists, wasn't it?

This grumpy old man is happy to spend the rest of his days here, wishing people would not say 'haitch' and feeling confused about gender intolerance. Years ago a friend and I mooted an imaginary organisation called the Society for the Preservation of Equal Rights for Men (S.P.E.R.M. for short). It was only meant as a joke then. Now it may amount to a Hate Crime.

The woolly-hatted, staring maniac at Number Ten is apparently going to allow Radio Four to continue its existence and I shall continue to listen to the station's brilliant documentaries, unless the added music becomes unbearably intrusive. Why do they add music? It baffles me. Is it supposed to make the programme 'more interesting'? Would listeners turn off, if there were no music? They'll be adding music to the News next.

And why do people start sentences with the word 'So' when there is no consequence involved? I am fine with, "The house was on fire, so I called the fire brigade." I am confused by: "Hello, Denise, welcome to 'Pointless, tell us all about yourself" "So, I'm a nurse."

"So, you're a nurse? As the result of what are you a nurse?"

I am all the things it is politically incorrect to be: English, male, white, middle-class, privately educated, from the Home Counties and heterosexual. There are probably more defects but I feel that here in NorthYorkshire I can hide those shortcomings from a complaining world, that is constantly demanding apologies for everything, including historical events that took place before any of us were born. If I survive this Coronavirus plague, I'll only have things like this to worry about: In order to make things more inclusive, should the Victorian poet, Gerard Manley Hopkins, be re-branded as 'Gerard Personally Hopkins'?

Acknowledgements:

My thanks to my sister, Ba, and Mike Guilbride for proof-reading, to Susie for her patience and to Diane Moss for saying, "You ought to write a book!".

Acknowledgements:

INDEX

Abse, Leo	129	Brown, Sandy	60
Aeolian Hall	57	Browne, Coral	152
Aicha, Lalla	81-82	Bruce-Lockhart, Logie	34
Aicha, Princess Lalla	81	Budd, Sir Alan	149
Albanians	74-75	Bush House	62-63
Albert Hall	73-74	Bywater Street	70-71
Ali, Muhammad	90	Cambridge Footlights	132
Ammonds, John	84	Cambridge Hawks	8, 39
Athena Society	33-34	Cartledge, Sir Bryan	110
Attenborough, David	64, 169	Cassels, John	60, 62
Attenborough, Sir David	169	Cavett, Dick	88
Auntie BBC	169	Charman, Colin	138
Auriol	131	Combined Cadet Force	29
Aylesford House	37-38	Commissioning Editors	136, 153
B. B. C.	15, 27, 57, 73, 78, 80, 105-106, 136-138, 140-141	Condren, Tim	114-115
B. B. C. Light Programme	15	Corcoran, Tom	119
Baker, Richard	102-103	Coronavirus	173
Barton, Dick	6, 15	Cotton, Bill Junior	64
Bates, Ralph	11	Cotton, Billy Senior	75
BBC Director General	98	Dalai Lama	87
BBC Television Centre	81, 87	Daniels, Paul	144, 148
BBC World Service	62-63	Davis, Sammy Junior	67
Beauclerk, Murray de Vere	23	Dee, Simon	65, 67, 81
Bickmore	8	Denison-Smith, Tim	7
Bird, John	45, 71	Dodd, Ken	115
Birt, John	59, 134-135, 137	Doodlebugs	2
Bluebell Girls	88	Dux, Liz	95
Booth, Chris	155	Ealing Film Studios	134
Botallack	11	Edmonds, Edward	13, 33
Botallack House	11	Ellington, Duke	91, 125
Boy George	108-109	Elton, Ben	132
Bradley, Richard	35	Eton College	16
Breeze, Chris	69	Eurovision Song Contest	73, 128
Briers, Richard	71	Evans, Edith	90
British Museum Reading Room	55	Fielding, Helen	127, 131
Broadmoor	96, 100	Forbes, Brian	83

INDEX

Forsyth, Bruce	68-69
Foster, Alfred	24
Freeman, Alan	64
Fry, Stephen	131-133, 156
Generation Game	68-69
Gladys, Castle Called	53
Good, Jack	70
Gorhambury	50-51
Gregson, Bob	62-63
Greyhound Bus	42-43
Grimston, Lady Romayne	52
Grimston, Viscount	51
Guilbride, Mike	53, 174
Hall, Tony	98
Hallam, Flight Lieutenant Toddy	1
Handl, Irene	71
Hardy, Sir Edward	3
Harris, Max	68
Hart, Chris	53, 61
Harvey-James, Arthur	16, 33
Harvey-James, Basil	16
Harvey-James, Stephen	11
Hatch, David	59, 64
Hawser, Lewis	128
Head of Light Entertainment	57
Hearn, Dan	40
Heavenly Productions	154
Henebery, Terry	75
Howe, Sir Geoffrey	110, 112
Humphrey, Sir	97
Hussey, Marmaduke	134
Inverlochy Castle	156
Ironside, Edmond	29
Ironside, Field Marshal Lord	29
Jacobs, David	79
James, Clive	171
James, Tony	74, 122-123
Jones, Bridget	127
Jones, Tom	89
Las Vegas	88-89
Laurie, Hugh	131
Lewes Operatic Society	159
Lipman, Maureen	84
Lloyd, John	131
Locke, Albert	159
Lollobrigida, Gina	91
Mallet, David	70-71
Mallet, Sir Victor	70
Malling, R. A. F. West	30
Malling, West	1, 30
Margaret, Princess	82-83
Marshal, Arthur	71
McAndrew, Daisy	95-96
McEnroe, John	107, 108
McGee, Debbie	144, 148
Mensa	14, 151-152
Mensa Variety Show	152
Milliard, Bruce	130
Mindel, David	79, 127-128
Modlyn, Monty	92-93
Moir, Jim	75, 144
Monotony Club of Gt Britain	60
Moore, Dudley	71, 123
Morris, Desmond	65-66
Muir, Frank	71
Mullard, Arthur	81
Newman, Nanette	82-83
Nimmo, Derek	88-89
Noble, Peter	66, 68
Novak, Kim	56
Oddie, Bill	96
Oxford English Dictionary	55, 71
Parkinson, Michael	89-91
Pearson, Ruth	119
Pickles, Wilfred	71
Pritchard, Hilary	128
Radio Light Entertainment	57

Rajan, Amol	140	Waterstone, Tim	36-37, 125
Ranzten, Esther	81	Wellesley, Jane	125
Reece, Mr Roger	77	Wellington	91, 125
Richard, Cliff	75	Wellington Port	125
Riley-Smith, Hamish	26	Wellington, Duke of	91, 125
Roffey, Graham	22	Westminster, Duke of	41
Salcombe	53	Wheldon, Huw	64, 136-137
Saloon, Crazy Horse	149	Whitbread	7-8
Savile, Jimmy	14, 92, 94, 96, 99-100, 119, 127	White Christmas	79
Savile, Johnny	100	White City	64, 138
Savile, Sir Jimmy	94	White Horse	102-103
Schofield, Philip	95	Whitehouse, Brian	75
Scrabble, British Mensa	14	Whitehouse, Mary	100
Serle, Chris	53, 81	Wilde, Kim	118
Sherrin, Ned	70-71	Williams, Kenneth	84-85
Simpson, N. F.	70	Williams-Thomas, Mark	94
Sloan, Tom	73-74	Willoughby, Holly	95
Smith, Dame Janet	98-99	Wilson, Sandy	31, 85
St Albans, Duke of	23	Wogan, Sir Terence	86
Stevenson, Albert	65	Wogan, Terry	87
Stockdale, Grant	45	World Service	62-63
Stribling-Wright, Gill	81	World Service, Head of	63
Stuart-Clark, Chris	19	Yalding	1, 7, 15, 77
Susie	19, 124, 144-146, 157-158, 174	Yardley Court	8, 15
Thatcher, Margaret	113, 134, 149		
Theroux, Louis	92, 96		
Thompson, Paul	8		
Titheradge, Peter	57		
Tonbridge School	8, 12, 17, 19-20, 159		
Took, Barry	137-138		
Unwin, Stephen	22		
Verulam, Lady	51-52		
Voice Realm	168		
Wakehurst Place	154		
War Memorial Fund	16-17		
Warner Brothers	45		
Waterstone	36-37, 125		

INDEX

BV - #0056 - 040520 - C0 - 229/152/11 - PB - 9781913425111